THE CHICAGO COMPANION TO TOCQUEVILLE'S

Democracy in America

The Chicago Companion to Tocqueville's

Democracy in America

James T. Schleifer

THE UNIVERSITY OF CHICAGO PRESS · CHICAGO AND LONDON

JAMES T. SCHLEIFER is emeritus dean of the library and professor of history at the College of New Rochelle and has been a visiting lecturer at Yale University and the University of Paris. He is the author of the award-winning book *The Making of Tocqueville's "Democracy in America"*; coeditor of *De la Démocratie en Amérique*, a critical edition in the Pléiade series; and translator of the four-volume historical-critical edition of *De la Démocratie en Amérique* edited by Eduardo Nolla.

The University of Chicago Press, Chicago 60637
The University of Chicago Press, Ltd., London
© 2012 by The University of Chicago
All rights reserved. Published 2012.
Printed in the United States of America

21 20 19 18 17 16 15 14 13 12   1 2 3 4 5

ISBN-13: 978-0-226-73703-4 (cloth)
ISBN-13: 978-0-226-73704-1 (paper)
ISBN-10: 0-226-73703-9 (cloth)
ISBN-10: 0-226-73704-7 (paper)

Library of Congress Cataloging-in-Publication Data

Schleifer, James T., 1942–
The Chicago companion to Tocqueville's Democracy in America / James T. Schleifer.
p. cm.
Includes bibliographical references and index.
ISBN-13: 978-0-226-73703-4 (hardcover : alkaline paper)
ISBN-10: 0-226-73703-9 (hardcover : alkaline paper)
ISBN-13: 978-0-226-73704-1 (paperback : alkaline paper)
ISBN-10: 0-226-73704-7 (paperback : alkaline paper)
1. Tocqueville, Alexis de, 1805–1859. De la démocratie en Amérique.   I. Title.
JK216.T648S34 2012
320.973—dc23
2011040731

♾ This paper meets the requirements of ANSI/NISO
Z39.48-1992 (Permanence of Paper).

To Blaz and Niko

CONTENTS

PART II
What Are Some of the Major Themes of Tocqueville's *Democracy*?

PART III
American Readings of Tocqueville's *Democracy*

PART IV
Tools for Use

ACKNOWLEDGMENTS

Most generally, I want to thank my colleagues, the international community of Tocqueville scholars, who over the years, at innumerable lectures, seminars, and conferences, have stimulated and enriched my understanding of Tocqueville and his great book.

More specifically, my deep appreciation goes to two individuals: my wife, Alison Pedicord Schleifer, who read many successive drafts of the *Companion*, offering valuable suggestions along the way about style and clarity and carefully proofreading each time for typos and other errors; and John Tryneski, my editor at the University of Chicago Press, who first suggested the idea of such a companion to me several years ago, waited patiently for me to complete other Tocqueville projects, and then, as I wrote, offered me the encouragement, advice, and prodding necessary to produce the kind of classroom-friendly and useful *Chicago Companion to Democracy in America* we both envisioned.

Of course, the following work is mine, and I take full responsibility for any weaknesses or failings.

INTRODUCTION

WHY READ ALEXIS DE TOCQUEVILLE'S DEMOCRACY IN AMERICA?

SINCE ITS PUBLICATION IN TWO PARTS IN 1835 AND 1840, Alexis de Tocqueville's *Democracy in America* has been widely hailed in France, England, America, and elsewhere as a brilliant analysis, not only of American politics, society, and culture, but also of modern democratic society as a whole. Such lasting praise should at the very least alert us to the potential value of the book and incline us toward thoughtful consideration of the author's message.

Tocqueville asserted that increasing equality (or advancing democracy) was the defining feature of modern society. He was also able to see and to trace for his readers how democracy on the march would influence all areas of society, civil and political, transforming the entire world, including to some degree the character and psychology of human beings.

Tocqueville, in the course of his book, offers a political program for sustaining democratic societies that are prosperous, stable, and free— democratic societies that might be called "healthy." Perhaps his more significant message for readers today, however, involves not his proposed solutions, but the questions that he posed. For example: What did democracy mean, and how would it transform society? What varieties of equality (and inequality) marked modern society? How could liberty be preserved in an age of equality? How could the individual (or a minority) be protected against concentrated power, wherever it might emerge in a democracy? Why were the liberties, the civil and political rights, of the individual important, and how could they be strengthened and preserved? How could democratic societies avoid extreme privatism, excessive materialism, and the decline of a shared civic life? How could they nurture cultural and intellectual creativity? In a democracy, how could a core of common values be sustained? What was the appropriate role of religion? How could a high level of political leadership be maintained? What kind of education was needed? And how—for good or for ill— would advancing democracy reshape the psychology of modern human beings? In the following pages, these and many other questions (as well as Tocqueville's responses) will be discussed.

From the outset, however, it is important to note that Tocqueville, in his time and ours, did and does not fit into party labels or strict political categories. He saw himself as a liberal of a new kind, declared that he was not a party man, prided himself (perhaps wrongly) on his impartiality, and called for "a new political science . . . for a world altogether new."[1] Nonetheless, although he professed to be impartial in his politics and balanced in his judgments, Tocqueville was not a man without the moral anchor of principle. He was grounded most fundamentally in his passion for liberty, and he proclaimed himself a partisan of democracy who recognized that democratic society, despite its flaws, was more just than the aristocratic society of the past.

From one perspective, Tocqueville's masterpiece, which took over eight years to complete, is a thoroughly French book, written by a Frenchman who was hailed as the second Montesquieu. Intended primarily for a French—not an American—audience, it was designed to suggest how France could become a free and stable nation in the age of democracy, and was built—in part—on French sources. *Democracy in America* was meant to bring essential lessons to France. But it is also a book about America and, more broadly, a study of modern democratic society. So as we read Tocqueville's *Democracy*, we already have three quite different subjects to consider: France, America, and democratic society writ large. Here, Tocqueville's complex purposes also begin to come into view. In the following volume we will explore more fully Tocqueville's own reasons for writing *Democracy in America*.

WHAT ARE THE PURPOSES AND
USES OF THE *COMPANION*?

The goal of this companion is to present as comprehensive and balanced an introduction to Alexis de Tocqueville's *Democracy in America* as possible. This volume is meant to serve as a relatively brief guide to Tocqueville's book for students and other serious readers, especially those who are encountering his work for the first time. The task is formidable.

During the past half century there has been an explosion in Tocqueville scholarship. More specifically, new editions and translations of *Democracy in America* have proliferated, especially during the last twenty years. Each of the many contemporary editions of *Democracy in America*, both full and abridged, has an introduction and other appropriate editorial apparatus. And several excellent, brief general introductions to Tocqueville's thinking and writing over his lifetime have recently appeared.[2] Yet surprisingly, no one volume, focused solely on Tocqueville's great book, written by one author, and presented with a single voice exists. So what follows is not intended to be a general introduction to the whole body of Tocqueville's writings, or a broad analysis of his ideas, theories, and beliefs. It is meant quite simply to be a guide to *Democracy in America*, a concise, but informative effort to orient the reader to Tocqueville's most famous work.

We will address the ways in which *Democracy in America* reveals the originality of Tocqueville's analysis of modern democratic society and demonstrates his significance as a writer and thinker. Tocqueville's basic arguments, his insights and convictions, on the one hand, and his errors and omissions, on the other, will be summarized. And, throughout the *Companion*, we will attempt to capture the essential message of Tocqueville's book, noting especially his own repeated efforts, in text, drafts, and letters, to set forth the core of his argument. We will also examine the enduring attraction of Tocqueville and his book since 1835 and ask how well his *Democracy* continues to help today's readers understand modern democracy, grasp its tendencies, and cope with its challenges. In the twenty-first century, does Tocqueville still have something to say to us?

Attentive readers will quickly notice, in the following pages, numerous citations drawn not only from the published text of *Democracy in America*, but also from the working papers of Tocqueville's book, especially the successive drafts, and from his letters. Why?

When we approach Tocqueville's great book, we have a singular advantage. Most of his working papers still exist and are available for study. Those manuscripts, which we will discuss in more detail later, include his travel diaries, letters, early notes and jottings, initial outlines and plans, successive drafts and variants, and even the original working manuscript, in Tocqueville's own hand. This happenstance not only distinguishes Tocqueville's book from almost all other major works of political theory. (Imagine if we had numerous drafts and a much-revised autograph working manuscript of any given title by Plato or Montesquieu.) But it also provides us with a rare treasure trove of materials that helps to give voice to the published version. Sometimes the layers of drafts and other closely related manuscripts clarify Tocqueville's themes and concerns and reveal his intentions in ways that are absent from the printed work. The working papers of *Democracy in America* allow readers to follow how the language, structure, and message of Tocqueville's book evolved, and how the author thought and wrote. They can, in short, assist readers as they engage and interpret the text.

Many of Tocqueville's letters are also useful for reading his *Democracy*. Penned before, during, and even after the writing of his book, they show, in his own words, his understanding of his purpose and essential message, and they often describe his thinking patterns and writing strategies. Later, as we examine Tocqueville's major themes, we will encounter various examples of such self-revealing correspondence.

To disregard all of these materials, when they exist, is needlessly to overlook valuable resources and to risk oversimplifying or misunderstanding Tocqueville's work. The layers of *Democracy in America* are, remarkably, still available for us to uncover and explore. With the published text of his book, they have much to teach and should not be ignored. The following volume was written with that premise in mind.

This companion is also intended to provide useful tools for readers. All quotations from Tocqueville's published text are drawn from the University of Chicago edition of *Democracy in America*, edited and translated by Harvey Mansfield and Delba Winthrop, which is one of the most widely used contemporary editions; and almost all citations are keyed to that edition. Only when a draft version not available in the Chicago text is quoted or cited does a reference to an alternative edition appear.

The following volume also includes a glossary of key terms from Tocqueville's *Democracy* and a guide to essential chapters and passages of his book. In each case, cross-references are provided to places where, in both the Chicago edition and the *Companion* itself, those terms are discussed or those segments are found. Provided as well is a brief list of suggestions for further reading. Readers will also find below, especially in the chapters on Tocqueville's major themes, specific references linking the discussion to portions of Tocqueville's text. Such precise connections can be somewhat misleading, because his major themes are not characteristically confined to particular chapters, but poke through unexpectedly in many places throughout his book. Nonetheless, such guides will enable readers to move more easily between segments of the *Companion* and parts of *Democracy in America*.

These devices mean that the *Companion* can be read in two very different ways. It can be approached, first, as an extended essay on the purposes and meanings of Tocqueville's book. But the volume can also be used almost as a work of reference; by using the guides and other apparatus provided, readers can easily focus on topics of special interest to them.

Perhaps the most basic purpose of this volume is to suggest how to read *Democracy in America*. But my working assumption as author is that there is no single correct way to read or interpret Tocqueville's masterwork. Each generation of readers has found in his book somewhat different lessons and made new discoveries about their own times and circumstances. Perennial timeliness assumes that there are many ways to read and understand a book and an author.

So, to return to our initial question, why read Tocqueville's *Democracy*? We already have a few possible responses. An enduring reputation for greatness; the ability to raise lasting questions of significance about society, culture, and politics; and the richness and complexity to be read by each successive generation as, in some ways, a contemporary and timely study; these should all count as we consider and evaluate the book in the following pages.

PART I

WHAT ARE
THE CONTEXTS
OF TOCQUEVILLE'S
DEMOCRACY?

1

Who Was Tocqueville?

WHAT ARE SOME ESSENTIALS OF
HIS LIFE AND BACKGROUND?

TOCQUEVILLE'S BIOGRAPHY IS ALREADY WELL KNOWN and eloquently recounted. Three full studies, as well as several short biographical sketches, exist.[1] Our purpose here is not to cover familiar ground about Tocqueville's life. Later, when we retrace, in summary, the American journey, briefly tell the story of how his *Democracy in America* took shape, and examine the unfolding development of the major themes of the book, we will inevitably be drawn into descriptions of Tocqueville's background, his private and public activities, and his personal beliefs, values, and attitudes. For now, however, we can lay out some essentials.

Born in 1805 into a family of the old nobility, Tocqueville grew up in a highly privileged and well-connected setting. In the mid-1780s, just before the French Revolution, Chrétien Guillaume de Lamoignon de Malesherbes, Tocqueville's maternal great-grandfather and the most illustrious of his predecessors, had held high office under the old regime and had championed reform. But once the Revolution took place and Louis XVI was put on trial, Malesherbes stepped forward to defend his king, an effort predetermined to fail. This magnificent gesture made Malesherbes himself a marked man. He was guillotined in 1794, a year after the monarch. Many other members of the family were also arrested and imprisoned, and several were executed.

Among the jailed were Tocqueville's own father and mother, who barely escaped the guillotine. The emotional impact of this story on Tocqueville and his family is hard to exaggerate. The suffering endured during the

Revolution was periodically recalled at family gatherings. Tocqueville's mother never fully recovered emotionally and psychologically from the ordeal of imprisonment, near execution, and loss of so many close family members. And Tocqueville himself inherited not only the model of his great-grandfather, but also a profound aversion to what he later called the *revolutionary spirit*: the recourse to violent means in order to achieve extreme political ends and the use of unchecked power, wielded unjustly by a few, in the name of the many.

The faith and attitudes of his tutor, the Abbé Lesueur, reinforced the influence on the young Tocqueville of a family circle profoundly conservative in politics and orthodox in Catholic faith. But if the old priest, Bébé, as he was affectionately called, had encouraged orthodoxy in his young charge, he had also quickly recognized Tocqueville's remarkable intellectual gifts and pushed him away from a traditional military vocation and toward a career in law.

Given such a background, how did Tocqueville, as a very young man in the 1820s, begin to move away from predictable family attitudes and opinions? Three possible explanations can be offered. During the Restoration (1814–1830), his father, Hervé de Tocqueville, served the re-established Bourbon monarchy as a prefect in several successive localities, including the city of Metz, where Alexis, in order to attend school, joined him in 1820. There, the son, sixteen years old, discovered in his father's library the works of the Enlightenment philosophers, notably Montesquieu, Rousseau, and Voltaire. The adolescent Tocqueville suddenly found his religious beliefs shattered and his social assumptions upended. An intellectual and moral crisis shook him out of inherited social, political, and religious positions.

Decades later, Tocqueville described himself at that moment as surrounded by "intellectual ruins," all truths overturned or shaken. Until he discovered these authors, he wrote, his mind was filled with "all kinds of notions and ideas which usually belong to another age. My life up to then had flowed in an interior full of faith which had not even allowed doubt to penetrate my soul. Then doubt entered, or rather rushed in with unheard-of violence, not merely the doubt of this or that, but universal doubt."[2] A revolution in beliefs, ideas, and attitudes had taken place in Tocqueville's mind.

Also at work in the 1820s was a second intellectual dynamic. The decade witnessed an especially vigorous social and political debate among conservatives, ultraconservatives, traditional liberals, radicals, and a new group of reformers called the *doctrinaires*. This creative group of intellectuals, most notably Pierre Paul Royer-Collard, François Guizot, and Charles de Rémusat, developed an original body of political and social thought and historical analysis that appealed in broad outline to Tocqueville and, as we will observe, left an imprint on his thinking and writing.

Finally, a third reason for Tocqueville's more independent course is possible. From 1823 to 1826, he studied law and, in 1827, began his legal career as a newly appointed *juge auditeur*. According to André Jardin, the author of the first full biography of Tocqueville, the French law schools had become liberal by the 1820s. Perhaps this political tendency also helped to push Tocqueville's thinking in new directions.

Whatever the political impact of pursuing a career in the law at that time may have been, the personal results for Tocqueville were significant. As a young lawyer he met and quickly formed a close and crucial friendship with one of his colleagues, Gustave de Beaumont. Less positively, he also found work in law dull, uninspiring, and not suited to his interests or talents. It was too restricted and detailed as a field, and it did not appeal to Tocqueville's imagination or to the expansiveness of his mind. Tocqueville irrevocably abandoned his legal career in 1832, not long after his return from the New World.

HOW WAS HE ABLE TO WRITE
SUCH A BRILLIANT BOOK?

When considering Tocqueville's life, yet another question almost invariably arises. How did he see so well, especially someone as young as Tocqueville, who was only twenty-six years old during his voyage to America and only thirty when he published the first portion of his *Democracy*? How to explain his astonishing insights about the American republic, in particular, and about modern democratic society, in general? Of course, there is no definitive response to this query. Clearly, Alexis de Tocqueville possessed highly unusual gifts and a brilliant mind. Was he simply a genius? Is that the best solution to the puzzle?

Tocqueville himself offered another answer. He believed that he straddled two worlds, one aristocratic, the other democratic, and existed within a nation undergoing a painful transition.

> People attribute either democratic or aristocratic prejudices to me. I might have had either had I been born in another century and another country. But the accident of my birth made it quite easy for me to avoid both. I came into the world at the end of a long Revolution, which, after destroying the old state, created nothing durable in its place. Aristocracy was already dead when my life began, and democracy did not yet exist. Instinct could not therefore impel me blindly toward one or the other. I lived in a country that for forty years had tried a bit of everything without settling definitively on anything, hence I did not easily succumb to political illusions. . . . In short, I was so perfectly balanced between past and future that I did not feel naturally and instinctively drawn toward either, and it took no effort for me to contemplate both in tranquility.[3]

With a foot in both camps, so to speak, and with exposure to all that France had attempted and endured for nearly half a century, Tocqueville felt himself uniquely positioned to observe dispassionately, to reason calmly, and to judge fairly. He may have overestimated his balanced interest and neutrality, but his own explanation of his ability to write such a book at least deserves our consideration.

WHAT KIND OF MAN WAS TOCQUEVILLE?

Without doing an exhaustive portrait, we can perhaps note a few essential characteristics. In a letter to his friend, Charles Stoffels, Tocqueville confessed to his own sometimes "melancholic disposition," a recurring "painful state of the soul" marked by sadness and dejection. To move beyond those feelings, Tocqueville recommended avoiding both deep disgust and excessive enthusiasm with life. "Life," he wrote, "is neither a pleasure nor a sorrow; it is a serious affair with which we are charged, and toward which our duty is to acquit ourselves as well as possible. I assure you, my dear friend, that whenever I have managed to view it in this way, I have drawn great internal strength from this thought. . . . I have felt that

I was less apt to be discouraged and that, not expecting too much, I was much more satisfied with reality."

In the same epistle, he added a telling admission about another of his beliefs.

> When I first began to reflect, I believed that the world was full of dem-
> onstrated truths; that it was only a matter of looking carefully in order to
> see them. But when I sought to apply myself to considering the objects,
> I perceived nothing but inextricable doubts. I cannot express to you, my
> dear Charles, the horrible state into which this discovery threw me. . . .
> I ultimately convinced myself that the search for absolute, *demonstrable*
> truth, like the quest for perfect happiness, was an effort directed toward
> the impossible. It is not that there are not some truths that merit man's
> complete conviction, but be sure that they are very few in number. Con-
> cerning the immense majority of points that it is important for us to know,
> we have only probabilities, almosts. . . . Thus, one must resign oneself to
> arriving only very rarely at demonstrated truth.[4]

Such a near-total rejection of absolute truths would not only remain one of Tocqueville's defining principles, but also mark the message of his *Democracy*.

Almost twenty-five years later, in two letters to Sophie Swetchine, he revealed still other personal characteristics. In one, he described a "vague restlessness and an incoherent agitation of desires [that] have always been a chronic malady with me." (Note that in the second part of the 1840 *Democracy*, Tocqueville would describe these same feelings as essentially democratic.)[5] And in the other, he disclosed his sense of a "sort of solitude among men." "You could not imagine, Madame, the pain and often the cruelty I experience in living in this moral isolation, to feel myself outside the intellectual community of my time and my country."[6] Maybe his stance was not so much a suspension between two worlds as the position of someone who felt chronically outside the currents that embroiled his contemporaries. If so, his place as a double outsider—to his own world and to America—possibly helps as well to explain his exceptional abilities as an observer.

So Tocqueville sometimes experienced deep melancholy, what he had once called a "sort of sickly sadness." Despite several lifelong friendships, he had a deep sense of loneliness, of standing apart from his own time and generation. This did not bode well for the political career he hoped to undertake. And he was persuaded that claims to absolute truth were exaggerated and probably false. Except in rare cases, only probabilities existed for him. He lived in a world of "almosts," of approximations. As we will see, such traits in belief and personality would color his *Democracy in America* in a variety of important ways.

2

How Was *Democracy in America* Written?

*Why Did Tocqueville Visit the United States
in 1831? And What Did He Do There?*

REVOLUTION BROKE OUT ONCE AGAIN IN FRANCE IN JULY 1830. Tocqueville took a required oath of allegiance to the new constitutional monarchy of Louis-Philippe. But to free himself from a professional and political position that remained uncomfortable and ambiguous, Tocqueville proposed, with his new friend and fellow lawyer, Beaumont, to undertake for the French government an official mission to the United States to study the American penitentiary system. France badly needed prison reform, and the United States was then at the forefront of improvements. Their proposal was accepted, and the two young men completed the project in good faith. The mission truly served, however, first, as an excuse to escape, and second, as a pretext for an enterprise of a different sort. Tocqueville and Beaumont arrived in the New World with two projects to pursue: a governmental report on the penitentiary system and a self-assigned broader study of the American republic.

Tocqueville and Beaumont left France with the intention of traveling for about one year in North America. By November 1831, however, the government shortened their leave and insisted that they return in February 1832. So, in the end, the companions traveled for nine and a half months in North America, including two weeks in Canada. They left France on April 2, 1831, arriving in Newport, Rhode Island, on May 9. And on February 20, 1832, they departed from New York bound for Europe. There is no need here to retrace Tocqueville and Beaumont's travels in detail.[1] We can, however, summarize their itinerary and describe their journey to America in broad strokes, noting especially a few unexpected developments and some basic features of their visit.

Tocqueville and Beaumont spent about half their time in a few of the large cities of America: New York, Boston, Philadelphia, Baltimore, and Washington, DC. They also stayed for several days in Pittsburgh, Cincinnati, Louisville, and New Orleans. (A projected visit to Charleston, South Carolina, never took place.) Part of their travel was dictated by the need to visit important American penitentiaries and correctional institutions, most notably Sing Sing, on the Hudson; the Auburn prison, in upstate New York; and the Eastern State Penitentiary in Philadelphia.

So their journey was largely urban and northern, but with significant excursions across New York state and the Great Lakes to the Michigan frontier; up the Saint Lawrence to Montreal and Quebec City; down the Champlain valley and across Massachusetts to Boston; from Boston to Philadelphia, via Connecticut and New York; across Pennsylvania to the Ohio valley; down the Mississippi to New Orleans; a hurried return overland, across the South, to Washington, DC; and finally back to New York for their departure.

Their intended trajectory was deflected in several important ways. First, as we have already noted, the planned voyage was shortened at the demand of the French government. Second, last-minute decisions, made on impulse in July and August 1831, to go to the frontier (in Michigan) and then to visit the upper Great Lakes considerably changed their itinerary. And finally, several unforeseen circumstances influenced the course of their journey, including a steamboat accident and an extremely harsh winter in 1831–1832; the Ohio and parts of the upper Mississippi River froze, temporarily halting all steamboat traffic and trapping the two friends in dangerous cold in Kentucky and Tennessee. On the one hand, Tocqueville and Beaumont's firsthand introduction to the American frontier, including the character of the pioneer and the relentless nature of the westward movement, deeply enriched their experience.[2] On the other hand, the unexpected events that plagued the two travelers cut short their time in the South, creating a serious and unfortunate imbalance in their exposure to America.

As we will see, to sense the full flavor of Tocqueville and Beaumont's

journey, readers should consult Tocqueville's travel diaries, as well as the
letters written by the two companions to friends and family at home.[3]
Their experience in the New World cannot be adequately reconstructed or
fairly judged simply by looking at Tocqueville's *Democracy in America.*

How Did Tocqueville and Beaumont Work?

Tocqueville described the two companions as the "most implacable investigators."[4] Thanks to their official status, they found all doors open to
them. "Perhaps no one," he wrote to his brother, Edouard, "has ever been
better situated than we are to study a people. . . . We have regular contact
with all classes of society. We are supplied with all the documents anyone
could wish for. Finally, our purpose in coming here was purely serious.
Our mind has been focused steadily on the acquisition of useful knowledge. The labor is immense but not arduous, because in a way we are
soaking up ideas through every pore, and we learn as much in a drawing
room or on a walk as we do when closeted in our studies."[5]

This very early letter to Edouard captures much of Tocqueville and
Beaumont's characteristic methods of research. In addition to hinting at
their work routine and daily visits and activities as travelers and investigators, Tocqueville touches on perhaps the most essential feature of their
journey: contact with Americans. He recorded conversations with over
two hundred individuals, some named, some anonymous, some famous,
some obscure. And, by and large, the conversations were well planned
and deliberate, more interviews or managed dialogues than casual exchanges. Together Tocqueville and Beaumont framed initial questions to
raise with their hosts. As they traveled and learned more, they developed
new topics to explore, but returned methodically as well to familiar queries. Their conversations became a process of discovery, a way for them to
follow up on earlier remarks, ideas, and information and a means to test
their own developing opinions and insights.

Their joint impulse toward planned questions even led to a pioneering
research effort, undertaken as part of their official mission. In October
1831, in Philadelphia, they conducted interviews with numerous prisoners at the Eastern State Penitentiary, also known as the Cherry Hill
prison. The manuscripts of those interviews still exist and show a detailed

exploration by Tocqueville and Beaumont not only of the strengths and weaknesses of the system at Cherry Hill, but also of the causes of crime.

More generally, we should note that doing research on the penitentiary system—including visits, interviews, readings and periodic reports—helped to shape Tocqueville's portrait of America and informed his *Democracy*. Studying prisons, the behavior of prisoners and guards, the causes of delinquency, and the various American correctional philosophies led him to consider how crime was linked to issues of poverty, recurring economic crises, public education, treatment of juvenile offenders, racial inequalities, and social reform. Even more broadly, examination of the competing penitentiary systems in the United States suggested larger themes of the dangers of individual isolation and how association among individuals spurs communication and concerted action. Tocqueville's official mission cannot be divorced from his larger American experience.

Afraid of forgetting what they learned from a particular experience or conversation, Tocqueville and Beaumont kept pocket notebooks, small bundles of several sheets of paper, folded in half and secured with a straight pin. These pocket diaries, always at hand, allowed them immediately to jot down the essentials of a conversation, a key experience, or the germs of an idea.

At the end of each day, closeted in their rooms, they compiled more elaborate travel diaries, some arranged chronologically, others by topic, either randomly or alphabetically. Tocqueville devoted one compilation entirely to American civil and criminal law. In these notebooks, the two friends recorded more complete and detailed versions of their conversations, along with their developing opinions and ideas about America. Tocqueville's alphabetic notebooks, in particular, included increasingly substantive short passages of reflections that strikingly foreshadowed his *Democracy*. Part of their writing time was necessarily consumed by required periodic reports to Paris on their prison mission. But Tocqueville still was able to take detailed notes on important books that he had purchased along the way, most notably an 1831 edition of *The Federalist Papers* and James Kent's four-volume *Commentaries on American Law*.[6]

To accompany these travel notebooks as records of their journey, Tocqueville and Beaumont also wrote lengthy, elaborate letters home. Tocqueville specifically asked his family and friends to keep his letters; he intended to use them later when he began to draft his American book. Unfortunately, Beaumont's travel notes have been lost, but his letters survive and demonstrate how closely the two friends shared their work and approach as investigators and their ideas and impressions as travelers. Reflections and observations sent home in letters by the two friends are remarkably parallel and testify to a constant intellectual exchange.

As the existing travel papers show, the two companions also gathered books, documents, and a mass of other printed sources during their journey. In addition, Tocqueville, in letters home, asked a few friends and family members to write brief essays about the French administrative and judicial systems, or to describe French preconceptions of the American republic. He also requested from Jared Sparks,[7] whom he met in Boston, a written account about towns in America. He felt that he needed more information to guide his thinking about the extremely decentralized administrative structure that he was encountering in the United States.

To Le Peletier d'Aunay, one of those who received a request for a special essay, Tocqueville wrote:

[We] daily become more aware of the fact that the Americans and the French are guilty of opposite excesses. At home people complain of the abuse of centralization; here, the government is not evident at all, and, despite what people say, things are not always the better for it. Seldom do we find a general idea guiding a project undertaken in the public interest; one searches in vain for the central point from which an administration might set its course. . . . Some of our investigations have yielded fairly clear findings. This is the case when we know enough about the state of affairs in France that we can clarify our thinking by way of comparison. . . . To confine our attention to matters of public administration, we can see in a general way that everything here is different. What is better here than in France, what is worse, and what is simply different?[8]

To address these questions, Tocqueville now wanted to know more about "the state of affairs in France."[9]

In this letter Tocqueville focused on comparing France and America. But his journey notebooks also underscore comparison as an inescapable part of his method for clarifying his thinking. In his travel diaries he explicitly compared and contrasted the cities of New York and Boston; the English, French, and native inhabitants of Saginaw; the English and German stock of Pennsylvania; Ohio and Kentucky as free and slave states; the French of Louisiana and the French of Canada; and the North and the South.

What would result from nine months of travel and all of this effort? Tocqueville himself was not entirely sure. He recognized the challenge facing him and knew some of the weaknesses of his preparations, but he remained hopeful.

> I am leaving America, having used my time here in a useful and agreeable way. I have only a superficial idea of the south of the Union, but to know it as well as the north, I would need to spend six months there. Broadly speaking, two years are necessary to form a complete and accurate picture of the United States. Nevertheless, I hope that I haven't wasted my time. I'm bringing back a good many documents. I have talked and dreamed a good deal about what I have seen. I think that, when I return, if I have some free time, I might be able to write something passable about the United States. To embrace the whole thing would be madness. I cannot aspire to universal precision: I haven't seen enough for that. But I think I already know more about this country than we are ever taught in France, and certain aspects of the picture may hold great interest.[10]

The book that eventually emerged from the American journey would be considerably more than passable.

What Is the Importance of Tocqueville's Travel Diaries and Letters Home?

Tocqueville's own record of his American journey provides a key not only to reconstructing his travels, but also to understanding his *Democracy*. His journey notebooks and letters home serve as useful lenses for reading his book. They retrace his consideration of central themes, from first impressions to more mature and informed reflections, and reveal his methods for probing topics of interest, framing questions, choosing books, gathering printed documents, requesting help from others, and recording information and lessons gleaned by conversations, observations, and readings. They also disclose some of his key sources, including individuals and books, especially *The Federalist Papers* and the legal commentaries of James Kent. In short, they show Tocqueville as traveler, interrogator, researcher, and thinker.

Because they are more directly tied to specific experiences, conversations, and readings, his notes and letters are also more immediate, sometimes offering a more vivid version of a particular slice of America than the published account. By revealing the empirical background, providing the evidence, and exposing the germs of much of what he would discuss in his book, these journey documents also disclose more of the substance behind his textual analysis. Moreover, in Tocqueville's travel diaries, an attentive reader will find entries, especially some written toward the end of his voyage, that provide either elaborate and illuminating summaries of ideas that would appear in his *Democracy*, or entire passages that he would transport directly almost verbatim to his text.

Perhaps unexpectedly, Tocqueville's journey notes and letters also present a portrait of America different in some significant ways from the picture that would appear in his published work. The accounts written during the actual voyage are sometimes more nuanced. In the 1831–1832 materials, for example, Tocqueville says more about American inequalities, especially of wealth and race. He is perhaps more blunt and negative about the character and behavior of Americans, especially their greed and racism. And he is much more open in his praise for republican institutions, views he had to trim for his French audience. In his American papers, he discusses economic and technological developments in the United States far more. Even the important topic of education in democracies receives far more attention from Tocqueville in the diaries and letters he wrote while in the New World. Later we will examine some of the reasons why, in his book, he deemphasized or retreated into near silence about some of these topics.

What Were the Weaknesses of Tocqueville's Journey?

What single voyage would be truly adequate for grasping the whole of a nation and a people? In his letters home, Tocqueville acknowledged the weaknesses of his own American experience. He knew, in particular, that his journey had been too short and that he had hurried through the South. He fretted about his ability to digest the trunkloads of printed materials that he had accumulated during his travels. He also recognized where the gaps in his own knowledge were found, where doubt and missing information made it difficult for him to reach conclusions, and where he would have to choose among competing interests and themes.

Nonetheless, what Tocqueville experienced and learned in America is impressive. Four immediate tests of the distinctive quality of his American journey come to mind. First, out of his voyage, at least in part, came *Democracy in America*, a masterpiece of political theory. Second, with the exception of the work of one or two equally, or almost equally, perceptive commentators from abroad, Tocqueville's analysis of American society, culture, and politics stands far above that of any other foreign visitor. Third, without even considering the individuals that Tocqueville met in America or the extent of his travels, a full bibliography of his printed American sources in itself demonstrates the thoroughness of his research and breadth of his knowledge.[11] And fourth, setting Tocqueville's portrait of the New World republic—as found in his travel notebooks, letters, working papers, and published text—against current thumbnail sketches of Jacksonian America highlights the degree to which Tocqueville got America.[12] Tocqueville made mistakes, some serious, left things out, and suffered from his own prejudices and blind spots. Yet what he understood and wrote about the American nation and people continues to strike readers as uncannily perceptive.

A kind of shorthand critique of Tocqueville's American journey exists wherein a specific failure becomes emblematic of a gross weakness. Three complaints, in particular, are frequently made.

Complaint number 1. While in Boston, Tocqueville did not visit Lowell to see the emerging factory system. Out of this error, significant enough, arises the charge that he lacked any interest in industrialization or economic matters in general. Even more broadly, he is accused of ignoring the material basis of American society.

Later we will examine Tocqueville's economic ideas in more detail. But here we can note in passing that, as his travel notebooks, letters, and

other papers demonstrate, Tocqueville in America encountered the problem of poverty, recognized the existence of the poor within democratic
society, repeatedly noted the existence of classes and social and economic
inequalities, discussed the rapid growth of cities and the rise of manufacturing, and realized that industrialization led to "inequality arising from
the accumulation of personal wealth" and created "larger individual fortunes in America now than sixty years ago."[13] He was even aware that in
the South early efforts were being made to use slave labor in factories, a
southern twist on the rising factory system. And if Tocqueville didn't visit
Lowell, he did see Pittsburgh, which the two companions labeled "the
Birmingham of America."

More broadly, Tocqueville wrote perceptively in his diaries and letters
home about the impact on American prosperity of new technologies and
the construction of vast transportation and communication networks.
He repeatedly recorded details about canals, roads, and railroads, and
even noted the costs for operating a steamboat. Such "internal improvements" fascinated him, and he was quick to see their economic importance. Tocqueville also discussed with many of his hosts and experienced
firsthand the taming of the wilderness, the exploitation of resources, the
rush westward, the pushing aside of the non-Anglo-American populations, and the insatiable expansionism of American society. So he understood the transformation of America then underway, not only economi-
cally, but also geographically. As we will later observe, the rapid change
and tumultuous movement in America became, for Tocqueville, one of
the defining features of democratic society.

In his journey notes, as well as in his *Democracy*, Tocqueville always
carefully and faithfully listed the resources and physical circumstances
of America among the reasons for the prosperity and social and political success of the republic. His writings, it can be argued, reflect a vivid,
almost visceral awareness of the material basis of the United States. It was
no mystery to him.

Complaint number 2. Tocqueville and Beaumont went too rapidly
across the South, a fault that Tocqueville himself knew and regretted.
But because of this failing, Tocqueville is charged with not really understanding the South and with presenting an essentially northern or, more

specifically, a New England, perspective. There is considerable truth in this criticism; if any single place or experience in the New World can be identified as most influential for Tocqueville's thinking, Boston and the three weeks he spent there would be the candidate.

But readers need to recall that Baltimore and Washington, DC, were southern cities. The national capital even boasted a flourishing slave market. Tocqueville talked with several southerners whom he met outside of the South and with several wealthy planters with large holdings of slaves, including Charles Carroll in Maryland. He briefly visited a sugarcane plantation, commenting on its economics. And if he didn't go to Charleston, he at least gained an impressive command of the details, arguments, and passions of the nullification controversy, writing perceptively in his *Democracy* about the constitutional views of John C. Calhoun.[14]

But questions admittedly remain. Do his numerous discussions of the history and social, political, economic, and moral condition of the South, his analysis of how slavery shaped the South and southerners, and his treatment of the increasing tension and suspicion between North and South in the Union indicate a misapprehension? Or does Tocqueville show remarkable perspicacity? Ultimately, it is for readers to weigh the merits of what appears about the South in his published text.

Complaint number 3. Tocqueville spoke mostly with local notables, members of a social, economic, and political elite, particularly lawyers, judges, and political figures. From this observation comes the assertion that his circle of contacts was narrow, intensely elitist, anti-Jacksonian, and not at all representative of America or its democracy. Once again, there is undeniably some truth to this complaint. But part of this criticism arises from an idea that, for Tocqueville, issues of poverty, class, and social and economic inequality were invisible. And, as we have just noted, this assumption is mistaken. Moreover, Tocqueville's American acquaintances were not so few or limited as sometimes presumed. Carefully examining his journey notes, in particular, alerts readers to the number and variety of his informants, many of whom, although unnamed, provided valuable information and ideas. And among the prominent and named, not all were anti-Jacksonians; Edward Livingston and Joel Poinsett come to mind. More significantly, as one of today's preeminent historians of Jacksonian America has pointed out, the social and political opinions of Americans were complicated and not easily pigeonholed as Jacksonian and anti-Jacksonian, particularly at a time when political parties and identities were in flux.[15] Especially among local elites, views were highly nuanced and did not fit neatly into two blocs. So the charge against Tocqueville of political and social bias within the complex range of American opinion remains contestable.

None of this discussion about common criticisms is meant to deny significant failings or blind spots in Tocqueville's portrait of America; we will examine a few of those weaknesses again later. But some of the frequently made charges need at least to be challenged.

Tocqueville's Intellectual Encounter with America

As we will observe, Tocqueville arrived in the New World with much of the framework of his *Democracy* already in mind. On at least one occasion, Tocqueville himself described his ideas as largely formed before his American experience and presented his voyage as merely an opportunity to test his opinions about democracy. But he admitted as well, "[In the United States] I also saw several [things] that vividly illuminated my thinking. I discovered facts that struck me as useful to know."[16]

So if Tocqueville came with some expectations and notions already in mind, he also found himself, like most thoughtful and observant travelers, entertaining ideas and asking questions in America that he did not anticipate. His journey was, in part, what a current-day traveler has called a "process of unintended discovery." Tocqueville's intellectual encounter with the American republic cannot be ignored. At least on some matters, as we will see when we examine some of the major themes of Tocqueville's *Democracy*, it "vividly illuminated [his] thinking." The nine-month voyage in the New World made a difference.

Tocqueville's letters, in particular, express the mental commotion caused by his visit to America. To Ernest de Chabrol, he declared in June 1831, "I am quite simply dazed by all I see and hear."[17] And this message of intellectual shock persisted. From Boston in October 1831, he wrote again to Chabrol, asserting, "My brain here is in a constant ferment."[18]

So intense was Tocqueville's reaction to America, he had to remind himself not to be entirely captivated by the American model. "You see," he wrote to Louis de Kergorlay,

> that I am giving you the most thorough account I can of all the impressions I am receiving. In short, they are more favorable to America than they were during the first days after my arrival. . . . The principles of government are so simple, the consequences are deduced from them with so perfect a regularity, that the mind is subjugated and carried away if it does not take care. It is necessary to take stock of oneself, to struggle against the current in order to perceive that these institutions, which are so simple and so logical, would not suit a great nation that needs a strong internal government and fixed foreign policy; that it is not durable by its nature; that it requires, within the people that confers it on itself, a long habit of liberty and of a body of *true* enlightenment which can be acquired only rarely and in the long run. And after all that is said, one comes back again to thinking that it is nonetheless a good thing and that it is regrettable that the moral and physical constitution of man prohibits him from obtaining it everywhere and forever.[19]

If Tocqueville's encounter with America exerted a powerful pull and changed his ideas in certain ways, it did not solve all dilemmas or definitively settle all his opinions. Near the end of the journey, he confided to his father, "Just now I am mulling over many ideas about America. Many of these I am still turning over in my mind. A fair number have been set down in embryo and in no particular order on paper or remain scattered throughout the notes I made of my conversations after returning home in the evening [his travel diaries]. You will see all of these preparatory exercises. . . . I have thought a great deal about what could be written about America. To attempt a full portrait of the Union would be quite impossible for a man who has spent only a year in this vast country. . . . By being selective, on the other hand, one might present only topics more or less directly related to our social and political state. . . . That is the general framework."[20] As we will see, the story of the writing of his *Democracy*, what has been called his second voyage to America, would largely be a process of completing these "preparatory exercises," of making his selections among possible topics, and, most essentially, of continuing his reflections.

TOCQUEVILLE'S SECOND VOYAGE TO AMERICA

How Did Democracy in America *Take Shape?*

The making of Tocqueville's *Democracy in America* during the 1830s involves two separate but closely interwoven stories. The first concerns the actual writing of the 1835 and 1840 portions of his text: early planning, the organization and rereading of travel notes and letters, continuing research, actually putting pen to paper, the establishment of a work routine, reactions to comments from family and friends on successive drafts, ongoing revision, and, especially after 1835, the broadening scope and changing timetable of his work.

The second narrative includes all of Tocqueville's other activities, involvements, and writings during the decade when his *Democracy* was taking shape and serves as an inescapable context for the writing of his book. Especially after 1835, events in Tocqueville's life, including bouts of illness, help to explain the slow completion of the second half of his work. But his other activities during the 1830s—completion, with Beaumont, of their study of the American penitentiary system; travel, especially to England; the writing of additional essays, articles, and reports, including those on pauperism, on France before the Revolution, on Algeria, and on the abolition of slavery; wide reading; conversations in person and by letter with a growing circle of acquaintants; and pursuit of political campaigns and projects—did not simply delay his book. They also provided Tocqueville with new experiences, information, and perspectives and suggested additional ideas and topics of interest that would enrich and modify the drafting of his *Democracy*. A more detailed recounting of what has been called Tocqueville's second voyage to America can be found elsewhere.[21] But we should note here several essential features of Tocqueville's almost decade-long process of thinking and rethinking, writing and rewriting.

Tocqueville's Working Papers

During the 1830s Tocqueville accumulated a large collection of working papers for his *Democracy*. From his journey to America, he already had numerous travel diaries and letters home. In October 1833, when Tocqueville finally began work in earnest on his American book, he made a preliminary list of sixty-four topics that he considered essential. Then, gathering his notebooks and letters and using that listing, he developed an index to those initial working materials, which he labeled his *sources manuscrites*. Some entries in the index were specific, such as Banks, Canals, Press, Roads, Tariff, Town-Meeting; others were basic organizing themes, such as Centralization, Equality, Sovereignty of the People, Public Opinion, Federal Organization, Union (future), and General Character of the Nation. And, to supplement the books, pamphlets, and other materials that he had brought home from America, he compiled and briefly annotated bibliographies of additional printed sources on such topics as Statistics and Generalities, Historical [works], Books on law, Legislative documents, and Indians. As a researcher, Tocqueville's preparations were impressive.

His first efforts, in addition to plans, guides, and outlines, included jottings on French and European history that would eventually become his eloquent introduction, and notes drawn from his extensive collection of books and documents on American colonial history that would serve as the base for his second chapter, "On the Point of Departure and Its Importance for the Future of the Anglo-Americans."[22]

As he began his actual draft, he lightly creased each blank page in half lengthwise, creating a right-hand side, where he could compose, and a left-hand side, initially left clean, where he could put outlines or sketches to guide his thinking, or insert queries and comments made by himself or by later readers, or write corrections and revisions. His manuscript quickly became dense with cross-outs, interlinings, alternative fragments, symbols, and accumulated comments, marginalia, and questions of many kinds.

So the "second voyage," that is, the making of Tocqueville's *Democracy*, saw the piling up of a rich hierarchy of sketches, reflections, notes, indexes, outlines, and successive drafts, culminating in a heavily annotated and corrected original working document, written in his own hand. As we have noted, most of those papers still exist to help us read and understand his book.

Help from Others

As he wrote, Tocqueville not only constantly reconsidered his ideas and revised his drafts. He also habitually sought out the reactions and advice of a small group of family and friends. Despite a certain reputation for having a rather cold and distant personality, Tocqueville carefully nurtured and treasured a small circle of close friends, especially Louis de Kergorlay, a close friend since childhood, and Beaumont. Kergorlay, more conservative than Tocqueville, often challenged the latter's ideas, forcing Tocqueville to clarify his positions and to rethink his arguments. Kergorlay also apparently brought greater moral sensitivity to their discussions, often urging Tocqueville to highlight the moral dimension of an argument or to opt for a strategy of writing from the highest possible perspective. His mark is found in many places in Tocqueville's *Democracy*.

Gustave de Beaumont, as Tocqueville's most trusted critic, made an even more profound impact on his book. As various scholars have argued, Tocqueville and Beaumont can perhaps best be understood as an intellectual and even authorial pair. They complemented each other's personalities and, except for a brief period in the 1840s, remained lifelong friends. When both were young lawyers beginning their careers, Beaumont, who was three years older, served as something of a mentor to Tocqueville. In the New World, they became inseparable traveling companions, following the same methods of conversation and note taking, comparing daily their observations, information, and ideas as they visited the American republic (and later traveled together in England and Ireland). They collaborated closely on their American books of 1835, intended to be companion pieces: Tocqueville's 1835 *Democracy* and Beaumont's *Marie, or Slavery in the United States*.[23] And they continued to serve as essential readers and critics for their post-1835 works: Tocqueville's 1840 *Democracy* and Beaumont's *L'Irelande sociale, politique et religieuse*, published in 1839.

During the summer and fall of 1834, Beaumont, whom Tocqueville called "my judge," heard or read the entire draft of the 1835 portion, putting many of his reactions in writing. Also invited to read a legible copy of the entire manuscript were Tocqueville's father, Hervé de Tocqueville, and his brothers, Edouard and Hippolyte. In addition, Kergorlay read and reacted in writing to the 1835 introduction. Always methodical, Tocqueville collected and arranged their responses in yet another manuscript document, and then used their questions and suggestions to revise his manuscript a final time.

For the 1840 portion of Tocqueville's book, Beaumont, Kergorlay, and a few other chosen readers again provided reactions and commentary, but mostly face to face, rather than in writing. Although his brother Edouard continued to serve as a useful listener and judge, Tocqueville longed for his most trusted advisers. As he wrote, he told Beaumont, "I lack only a good instrument of conversation. I need either you or Louis. The system would then be perfect." Tocqueville told Kergorlay much the same: "[Many] ideas remain obscure in my mind because it is impossible where I am to throw them out in a conversation with you and see how you set about to combat them, or, accepting them, how you give them a new twist. There are three men with whom I live a bit every day, Pascal, Montesquieu and Rousseau. A fourth is missing: you."[24]

In October 1838, Tocqueville finally completed a full but still preliminary draft of the 1840 *Democracy*. For about three months, a first great rereading and revision took place, with Kergorlay at Tocqueville's side acting yet again as instrument of conversation and judge. During this period, Tocqueville, completely dissatisfied with the opening segments of his book, literally threw his first two chapters, over one hundred manuscript pages, into the fire. They would have to be entirely rewritten. He wondered if he should open the 1840 portion by discussing democratic individualism, a topic that seemed to be assumed in the chapters on sources of belief and public opinion.[25] Kergorlay advised against such a shift in the order of argument, persuading Tocqueville that the section on ideas began his book at an appropriate, elevated level. Kergorlay's influence had other consequences as well. The fate of one chapter in particular was left to him. Tocqueville could not decide whether to delete the segment or not. But Louis, Tocqueville noted, "thinks this piece must *absolutely* appear in the work."[26] The fragment under discussion was the famous chapter "Why Democratic Peoples Show a More Ardent and More Lasting Love for Equality Than for Freedom."[27] Without Kergorlay's insistence, the chapter may never have appeared.

In August 1839, Tocqueville returned once again with intensity to his great work, spending the next few months on a grand final revision. By November, his manuscript was ready for yet another review by his faithful readers. Tocqueville told Beaumont that the draft "would pass through your eyes or ears, as you wish, and you would be able to judge it all in one breath. I ask this last effort of your friendship." Shortly after, he noted, "You will see even on the manuscript some traces of the importance which I give to this task. You will find in many places phrases such as this one: *To include only after having read it to B.* [Beaumont] *and to L.* [Louis de Kergorlay]; or this other: *Propose these two versions to B. and to L. and make them choose.* Unfortunately, one of my two counselors is missing. So try to double your wisdom."[28] After this last pass by Beaumont, the work was finally ready. The help of his judges had been indispensable.

What Were the Sources of Tocqueville's Book?

Beyond acknowledging the personal and essentially private influences of his chosen circle of readers, it is perhaps an insoluble problem to identify the sources of Tocqueville's *Democracy*, in particular, and of his ideas, in general. What follows is not an attempt either to enumerate those sources, or, once catalogued, to link them precisely to Tocqueville's book, demonstrating definitively the influence of those sources on his ideas. The scope of this volume does not allow such ambitious goals. Instead we will examine the different categories of sources important to the making of Tocqueville's book and consider some of the significant contexts in which he thought and wrote.

Although sources and contexts overlap, they are not the same. Sources are usually understood as specific books, individuals, or experiences. Contexts have to do with the broader settings—historical, cultural, intellectual, religious, political, and even biographical—that help to mold the ideas and opinions, assumptions and questions, perspective and approach, in short, the mentality or intellectual orientation of a writer. Contexts, which are often clusters of individual sources, need to be recognized as influences of the first order on any author or book. Tocqueville and his *Democracy* are no exceptions.

To try simply to catalogue the great multitude of specific sources for Tocqueville's book would be a daunting task. But the rich variety of his sources can be more easily and usefully noted: the reading of books, pamphlets, and newspapers; attendance at lectures; travel to the United States,

Canada, England, and Ireland; direct observations and firsthand experiences; conversations; more formal interviews; ongoing dialogues in person and by letter; interactions with good instruments of conversation; work with research aides; the composition of other essays and reports; and political plans and projects. Most broadly, Tocqueville's sources, in addition to a wide array of other private and public activities, may be summarized as: engagement with printed materials; interaction with other individuals, from famous to obscure, from lifelong friends to passing acquaintances; and exposure to other countries that served as points of contrast and comparison. Later, as we examine the development of his major themes, we will encounter many of the specific sources that influenced Tocqueville's book.

But for grasping Tocqueville's thought, identifying the broader settings out of which *Democracy in America* grew is arguably as useful as trying to track down individual sources. We have already briefly noted two background stories essential to the making of his book: the account of Tocqueville's early upbringing, family recollections and models, growing separation from familial social and political norms, and career preparation; and the important influence of his other activities during the 1830s. Several additional contexts, both personal and public, now deserve our attention.

For an understanding of Tocqueville's book, the extended intellectual relationship between Tocqueville and Beaumont, especially during the 1830s, remains unavoidable. From the late 1820s to 1840 (and beyond), the two friends gathered information together, discussed and developed ideas, reached conclusions, planned their books, determined strategies for writing, exchanged and critiqued their drafts, refined their styles, suggested rewordings and alternative passages, and provided mutual encouragement as needed. Manuscripts and letters indicate that Tocqueville helped to write Beaumont's *Marie*, as well as his book on Ireland. And just as surely, Beaumont helped to draft *Democracy in America*. This quite remarkable collaboration is one of the fundamental frameworks for the making of Tocqueville's book.

We also need to recognize several significant historical or public settings for Tocqueville's work. Tocqueville wrote against the background of French history since 1789, including the Revolution's lofty beginnings, as Tocqueville understood them, the descent into the Terror and tyranny, the rise and fall of Napoleon, the establishment and collapse of the Restoration, the July Revolution, and the subsequent start of the July monarchy. This historical pattern, during the half century before the publication of *Democracy in America*, of repeated revolution, recurring despotism, changing regimes, and enduring social and political instability profoundly influenced Tocqueville's questions, reflections, judgments, and fears about the nature of modern society and politics.

Among historical and intellectual contexts for Tocqueville's book, perhaps the broadest is the long course of Western political thought, a tradition that he knew well. As we have seen, Tocqueville, by his own testimony, habitually read Pascal, Montesquieu, and Rousseau. But, as he drafted the 1840 *Democracy*, he broadened his readings considerably. As a researcher, he was always gathering, summarizing, and learning from books, pamphlets, and other printed materials; the abundant collection of publications he had assembled in America testified to that impulse. Fearing, however, that his own opinions would be somehow deflected by the views of others, he assiduously avoided reading any secondary works that touched directly on topics he was considering. But this persistent characteristic of refusing to read books closely focused on his topics of interest did not stop Tocqueville, especially after 1835, from reading and pondering more general works by imposing figures of literature, history, political theory, philosophy, religion, or science.

His letters and working papers reveal that between 1835 and 1840, in addition to authors already mentioned, he consulted classic works by Plato, Aristotle, Plutarch, Thomas Aquinas, Machiavelli, Montaigne, and Bacon. Among seventeenth-century French writers, he read Bossuet, Descartes, La Bruyère, Charles de Saint-Evremond, and Madame de Sévigné, and from the eighteenth century, Bernard de Fontenelle, Jean-Baptiste Massillon, Malesherbes (his own great-grandfather), and the *Encyclopédie*. He also read Rabelais, Cervantes, the Koran (on which he took extensive notes), and works by some of his contemporaries, especially Guizot, Dominique Lacordaire, and François Auguste Mignet. Tocqueville's dialogues, throughout his *Democracy*, with some of the leading figures of this tradition, especially Montesquieu, witness eloquently to the importance of this particular background. Perhaps Tocqueville's drive toward wide reading reflected the more abstract and theoretical direction in which the 1840 portion of his *Democracy* was moving.

Still another example of historical or intellectual context, one closer to Tocqueville's time, is the rich development of French political thought in the early nineteenth century, including the works of French liberals, like Benjamin Constant, but more especially the ideas of the doctrinaires in the 1820s, notably such figures as Pierre Paul Royer-Collard, Charles de Rémusat, and François Guizot. During the past three decades, various scholars have rediscovered and drawn new attention to this body of political theory, which constitutes one of the fundamental settings for Tocqueville's thinking and writing. From this more contemporary tradition, for example, came Tocqueville's developing awareness by the late 1820s of such fundamental issues as revolution; centralization; the march of democracy and the rise of the middle class; the meanings of republicanism, sovereignty and representation; liberty of the press; the possible abuses of unchecked power; and the future of liberty. Long before he sailed for the New World, the debates of the 1820s filled Tocqueville's mind with many of the questions and ideas that would be central to his book.

Developments during the early nineteenth century in France can be understood in a somewhat different way. Tocqueville was part of a particular generation. He shared the cultural and emotional orientation of a generational cohort that was aware of the erratic history and relative decline of their nation since 1789, and distrustful of many of the ideals that had been proclaimed by various voices at successive moments during that period. Many in Tocqueville's generation felt suspended between two worlds, an old society refusing to die and a new society still being born; caught in a time of transition; and forced to confront a society that was out-of-joint and torn apart by enduring social and political conflicts. Like many of his contemporaries, Tocqueville longed for social harmony, political stability, genuinely free institutions, and a sense of higher purpose. What might be called the mentality of his generation also needs to be acknowledged as a shaping force for Tocqueville's *Democracy*.

Even more specifically, the French political scene of the 1830s presented an important background for Tocqueville's thinking and writing. By the mid-1830s, Tocqueville witnessed what he saw as the betrayal (once again) of the high ideals announced by political leaders at the moment of the July Revolution. And as the decade progressed, he observed unworthy leadership, a political life that lacked integrity, the absence of any higher vision, and growing materialism and self-interest. Despite his intense ambition to play a political role, he found himself disgusted by the politics of his day, which he judged profoundly immoral. As early as 1837, he laid out the path that he would essentially follow as a political figure until he withdrew from public life, nearly fifteen years later. From the beginning, rejecting much of the political scene around him, he tried to stand apart from existing parties and groups and to remain independent. At the core, he hoped to rally his own coalition, one of a new kind. His strategy remained largely unsuccessful and his hopes unfulfilled. But his perception of French politics colored especially the 1840 portion of his *Democracy*; it served as another important setting for his work.

The American experience stands as yet another key context for Tocqueville's thinking and writing. Of course, he did not arrive as a blank slate in the New World. To some degree, as we just noted, he had a conceptual framework already in mind. But in the working papers and text of his *Democracy*, Tocqueville repeatedly mentions moments of discovery or surprise during his American travels. His own language, as we have observed, indicates that America offered him unexpected lessons that deflected his thinking in significant ways. Preconceptions and settled elements in his thought were shaken. The nine-month voyage to the New World, it can be argued, modified Tocqueville's pattern of thought on some matters and provided him with important new insights and ideas. Our later discussion of his major themes will present several telling demonstrations of how the journey to America made a difference for Tocqueville and his book.

Much the same argument can be made for the importance of Tocqueville's visits to England in 1833, and to England and Ireland in 1835. Later, when we discuss Tocqueville's ideas, we will see noteworthy traces of the English context, broadly understood, on his *Democracy*. The second, longer voyage across the Channel, in particular, profoundly influenced

Tocqueville's thinking about the nature of aristocracy, centralization, industrialization, poverty, and social reform.

Finally, we need to point out yet another context, one easy to overlook. The 1840 *Democracy* took shape against the background of the 1835 portion of Tocqueville's work. The success of the first part (1835) set such an almost impossibly high standard for Tocqueville's labors on the second (1840) that he was often in despair. In many ways, the 1840 *Democracy*, as we will see, emerged from germs in the 1835 portion; but as we will also see, the gap in years between the two segments also meant that Tocqueville changed his mind or shifted his emphasis on some matters.

Recognizing the various contexts of Tocqueville's *Democracy* is essential for understanding his ideas. Some Tocqueville specialists emphasize the impact on his thinking and writing of one or more of the various French contexts, especially the long tradition of French political philosophers, or the political and historical thinkers of Tocqueville's own generation. Others stress the importance of what Tocqueville learned from his English voyages. Still others highlight the American framework of Tocqueville's book, the centrality of his journey to the New World as a time of surprises and discoveries that pushed Tocqueville's ideas and assumptions in new, unexpected directions. But giving a privileged place to one or another of these settings does not mean denying the significance of the others. Perhaps, as some commentators argue, *Democracy in America* can be profitably read simply as a text. But Tocqueville's book should also be read in context. Tocqueville wrote against a variety of biographical, historical, and intellectual backgrounds. These settings remain an inescapable part of the making of his work.

Acknowledging contexts solves only part of the puzzle of identifying what influenced Tocqueville's book. Another significant problem remains. Tocqueville often hid his sources. How can we discover them? A careful reading of the citations and appendixes presented in Tocqueville's own published text reveals, at least in part, the breadth and richness of his sources. But he warns his readers at the outset that he does not always identify individuals who served as important sources for him. To discover at least some of those silent sources, readers must resort to Tocqueville's travel diaries. In many cases, Tocqueville also dropped from his final text supplemental references to books (*The Federalist Papers*, for example) or authors (François Auguste Mignet, for example) that appear in his drafts or original working manuscript. And buried in the working papers of the last section of the 1840 *Democracy* are many newspaper clippings and notes on conversations with French political figures about contemporary economic and industrial issues. We know as well that Tocqueville relied, without any specific acknowledgment in his text, on help from those who wrote essays, at his request, about the French administrative system. And he remained silent about comments from his small circle of favored critics who read (or heard) his manuscript and suggested revisions of his ideas, arguments, and language.

If Tocqueville dropped from his text some citations that appear in his working papers and remained silent about some of the significant help he received from family and friends, he also suppressed his sources in more important ways. His intellectual encounters, especially with other major political theorists, are usually unacknowledged in *Democracy in America*. For example, although an explicit dialogue with Montesquieu about the role of fear and religion as supports for despotism takes place in the pages of Tocqueville's book, an even more extended reconsideration and revision of Montesquieu appears only in Tocqueville's travel notes and drafts of his book. And his intellectual conversations with Rousseau, Guizot, and Mignet occur in Tocqueville's published text without any specific acknowledgment. Demonstrating the impact on his *Democracy* of any given author or book remains largely a matter of recognizing parallel arguments, pointed responses, or special attention paid to particular topics of mutual interest. Only if a reader knows well the work of Pascal, or Bossuet, or Montesquieu, or Rousseau, or that of early nineteenth-century French political theorists such as Constant, Rémusat, Royer-Collard, or Guizot, can Tocqueville's intellectual engagement with these writers be spotted. For attentive readers such unspoken exchanges between Tocqueville and some of his sources are one of the most fascinating features of his work.

So although, in his text, Tocqueville specifically cites an impressive array of sources in notes and appendixes, he drops others from view. How to recover those and other hidden sources? Tocqueville's working papers (especially his travel diaries and drafts) disclose some. Others can be surmised by indirection, by the recognition of significant intellectual debts and dialogues. Still others remain forever elusive.

THE STYLE AND STRUCTURE OF TOCQUEVILLE'S *DEMOCRACY*

Tocqueville's Ways of Writing: How Does He Address His Readers?

At the outset, we need to recognize that for Tocqueville thinking and writing advanced together in a continual process of reconsideration and revision. His characteristic pattern of work resulted from a variety of causes, including chronic self-doubt, an impulse toward perfectionism in both language and order of argument, and a reluctance to stop at any given conclusion or judgment. Such an approach often caused him deep anxiety as he drafted his book. Nonetheless, it is possible to distinguish between Tocqueville's habits of mind (his thinking) and strategies of composition (his writing). When we examine the major themes of *Democracy in America* and retrace the development of many of Tocqueville's ideas, we will encounter some of his distinctive ways of thinking. But how did he go about crafting his text? What were his ways of writing?

The working papers of his *Democracy*, especially the successive drafts and the original working manuscript, demonstrate his acute self-awareness as a writer. The margins are peppered with reminders to himself about his central ideas and purposes, with questions and comments to himself about his choice of words, or the truth, accuracy, or pertinence of a given point or example, and with his reactions to suggestions by his circle of privileged judges. These marginal jottings offer, in short, a running critique by Tocqueville of his own emerging work. The manuscript pages also contain an ongoing and multilayered recasting of sentences and paragraphs. The evolving versions illustrate his search for the right word, for the most elegant expression, for the most persuasive order of argument.

As a writer he sought simplicity and clarity (what he called "common sense") and the most telling example or illustration. He believed that the most trivial observation, an item of clothing, the use of particular words, the smallest social convention could reveal to the astute traveler the entire social and political condition of a people. This concept of the essential interconnection of all aspects of society helps to explain Tocqueville's sometimes breathtaking leaps, especially in the 1840 portion of his book, from a single detail to a vast generalization.

We have already observed the crucial role of his small circle of critics. His judges did not always agree in their remarks, nor in any case did Tocqueville always follow their advice. But their careful listening, reading, and subsequent suggestions challenged and stimulated Tocqueville's thinking and writing; they reminded him of his purposes, offered opinions about materials to include or delete, and even on occasion provided alternative wording for Tocqueville to use. In many ways—made particularly clear in his drafts and working manuscript—his book is the result of his extended interaction with his good instruments of conversation, who helped to define his ways of writing.

Tocqueville's awareness of self was matched by his awareness of his audience. He knew his target. As already noted, his *Democracy* was intended primarily for French readers. Years later he admitted: "Although I very seldom spoke of France in [my book about America] I did not write a single page without thinking of France or without having France in a manner of speaking before my eyes. . . . I always began with the [United States] in order to bring out a contrast or an analogy with [France]. . . . The constant, unspoken comparison with France was in my opinion one of the main reasons for the book's success."[29]

Eager to persuade, Tocqueville, in his working papers, often reminded himself who his readers would be, what their ideas and assumptions were, and what they would understand and follow. He worried not only about boring or puzzling his readers, but also about losing them. He carefully avoided saying anything that would push his readers into firm opposition to his views or drive them definitively away. For example, in response especially to his father's advice, he carefully rephrased passages that could be read as support for republicanism, because most of his intended French audience of the 1830s remained implacably hostile to the idea of a republic. Tocqueville also cut from his drafts any passages judged, upon rereading, too highly charged, too passionate or unrestrained. He strove constantly to strike a cool, detached, nonpartisan tone. He wanted neither to offend nor to appear as a party man.

Other strategies for persuading his readers were also carefully crafted by Tocqueville. He used tight syllogisms, expressed in closely connected paragraphs, sentences, or even phrases within long sentences, to carry his readers along, almost without their knowing, toward the point of view he wanted them to reach. This syllogistic and deductive flavor, grounded in taut, almost inescapable logical sequences, remains a hallmark of his *Democracy*.

A second favorite technique was indirection, beginning at an idea widely or easily accepted by his readers, and then guiding those readers, in a subtle way, along an intellectual path until they arrived where Tocqueville planned. He preferred not telling readers what he wanted them to think, but allowing them to come, as if by themselves, to the opinions he had in mind. He hoped that his readers, assuming self-discovery and sensing little direct effort by the author to tell them what to think, would willingly embrace his ideas as their own. Here was one of the strategies of his American book. This approach is, of course, disingenuous. The reader's road to truth is not really his own; it is a path carefully laid out and made smooth by an author acutely conscious of his own preparations and purposes. Once again, we see Tocqueville's self-awareness as a writer.

Tocqueville's efforts to carry his readers along indirectly to where he wanted them to be beautifully matched his purposes for writing his book. Of course his purposes—especially his political ones—were many, as we will see when we examine his major themes. But Tocqueville had at least four fundamental goals that we can mention here. With his book, he wanted to make himself known and launch a political career. He wanted to depict the American republic for interested readers. He wanted to describe and understand modern democratic society, including its tendencies, benefits, and dangers. And he wanted to instruct France in how to be stable and free. For this last purpose, in particular, the acceptance of his political proposals, of his new science of politics, of his liberalism of a new kind, required the effective persuasion of his French readers. Like Pascal, Tocqueville worked carefully to fit his methods of argument to what he understood to be the nature of his audience. By doing so, he hoped to capture their assent.

Two other characteristics of Tocqueville's writing deserve to be briefly noted here: his search for new words and his effort to define his terms. For both, we will encounter important examples later as we consider Tocqueville's major themes and ideas. But as he discovered the American republic and explored a democratic world entirely new, he felt compelled to seek (not often successfully) original words to describe what was novel. He also tried to define such terms as *equality, centralization, democratic despotism, revolutionary spirit*, and especially *democracy* itself. His working papers present many examples of working definitions and show him grappling, as he composed his *Democracy*, with the double challenge of teasing out all the subtle meanings of concepts central to his thought, and of writing in a precise and consistent way.

How Is Democracy in America *Organized?*

The University of Chicago Press edition and most other contemporary editions of Tocqueville's *Democracy in America* present the first portion of Tocqueville's book, originally published in 1835, as volume 1, and the second portion, published in 1840, as volume 2. What are now parts 1 and 2 of volume 1 in the UCP edition appeared in 1835 as two separate volumes. And the four parts of volume 2 also appeared in 1840 as two separate volumes, with parts 1 and 2 constituting the first, and parts 3 and 4, the second. Readers need to remain alert to these shifting formats.

Tocqueville's *Democracy in America*, as just noted, originally appeared in four volumes, two volumes in 1835 and two more in 1840. Neither this format nor this timeline always matched Tocqueville's intentions. Originally, he envisioned a very different sort of work.

Tocqueville and Beaumont came to the New World having already decided to write a book about America. They had apparently first conceived such a project sometime during the last half of 1830. Perhaps more significantly, the initial idea was to coauthor a joint study. On February 21, 1831, before beginning the journey across the Atlantic, Tocqueville wrote that the two friends were "leaving with the intention of examining in detail and as scientifically as possible all the mechanisms of this vast American society about which everyone talks and no one knows. And if events allow us the time, we expect to bring back the elements of a *good work*, or at least of a new work, for nothing exists on this subject."[30] That plan persisted into the first months of their journey, until, by late September 1831, as shown in their letters home, the shared work had become two separate books.

Two explanations for this division of labor are likely. The first involves a growing awareness of the immensity of their task, which Tocqueville once described as a constantly expanding circle. A decision to split the project in two would make the whole effort more manageable. The second possible reason to divide the work perhaps arose from Beaumont's developing fascination with issues of race in America. In the new design that emerged by October 1831, Tocqueville would write a book focusing on American laws and institutions. Beaumont would concentrate on American mores, particularly racial attitudes and behavior.

The Shape of the 1835 Democracy

See in vol. 1 (1835): Tocqueville's introduction, pp. 3–15; part 2, chap. 9, pp. 298–302, "Importance of What Precedes in Relation to Europe"; and chap. 10, pp. 302–96, esp. pp. 391–96, "Conclusion."

At first, Tocqueville faithfully maintained this focus on American laws and institutions. His initial, overall plan for what would become the 1835 portion of his book involved a tripartite design that echoed the analytic approach found in François Guizot's lectures, attended by Tocqueville in 1829: "*political society*—relations between the federal and state governments and [between] the citizens of the Union and of each state; *civil society*—relations of the citizens among themselves; [and] *religious society*—relations between God and the members of society, and of the religious sects among themselves."[31] This 1833 distinction between political and civil society would eventually emerge as the dividing line between volumes 1 and 2 of the 1835 *Democracy*. The third theme, religious society, would remain essential to Tocqueville's portrait of America and would eventually become the focus of several chapters or subsections (in both the 1835 and 1840 segments), but it faded as a separate and distinct portion of his book.

As Tocqueville's thinking about political society developed, he realized that the best way to organize the topic was to follow a basic premise of his argument. Since he believed that all American political institutions arose from the same principle, sovereignty of the people, first reflected in the towns, he decided to move from the principle, next to the town, then to the state, and finally to the Union, which he considered a resume of political principles and practices already found at the local and state levels. In 1835, his first volume faithfully reproduced this plan.

Tocqueville's draft moved rapidly ahead. He finished the first volume, largely on American political institutions, by the summer of 1834; and by the fall, still honoring the division of topics agreed upon with Beaumont, he plunged into volume 2. Although Tocqueville intended the second portion to concentrate on civil institutions, he continued to view them primarily through the lens of their political function. (Notable examples are the press, associations, and the jury.) Again, he sketched a preliminary outline that included most of the chapters in the second volume. Significantly absent from his plans, however, was any mention of the final long chapter on the future of the three races in America. That last portion of the 1835 *Democracy*, written late in the drafting of his book, though important, was essentially an addendum or appendix to Tocqueville's main text.

So we can think of the 1835 portion of Tocqueville's book as consisting of three segments: part 1, beginning with what Tocqueville called physical and historical circumstances, and then primarily addressing American political institutions; part 2, chapters 1 to 9, largely about American civil society; and the long, concluding section, part 2, chapter 10, "Some Considerations on the Present State and Probable Future of the Three Races That Inhabit the Territory of the United States," which discusses the then current situation and likely destiny of native and black, as well as white, Americans.[32] As part of that discussion, Tocqueville also treats the political, economic, and expansionist future of the United States. The chapter not only breaks out of the almost exclusive focus on Anglo-Americans that marks the earlier parts of Tocqueville's treatment, but also deals with matters of race and racism, of American racial attitudes, behaviors, and policies, topics that had previously been left mostly to Beaumont.

As a result of this late addition, what is labeled as "Conclusion" really serves to end only the final chapter, not the whole 1835 portion. The section originally intended by Tocqueville to conclude his 1835 work appears at the end of part 2, chapter 9, in the last subsection, entitled "Importance of What Precedes in Relation to Europe."[33] The language and argument of that segment, readers should observe, closely echoes Tocqueville's eloquent introduction; he once intended to close the 1835 circle of his thinking and writing in the last part of chapter 9. If he had, the 1835 *Democracy* would have been much shorter and, in many ways, far weaker.

His introduction must not be overlooked as the fourth key element of the 1835 *Democracy*.[34] Tocqueville's remarkable opening essay, one of the best known elements of his book, presents his fundamental thesis, discloses his central purposes, and sets the high moral tone of his entire work.

The first portion of Tocqueville's *Democracy in America*, in two volumes, finally appeared in January 1835. Tocqueville had written the first half of his masterpiece in a little over one year. The next two volumes, the 1840 portion, would take far longer to complete.

The Shape of the 1840 Democracy

The 1840 segment of his book ultimately appeared in two volumes. But when he returned to his American work in August 1835, Tocqueville initially planned to write only a single additional volume, focused primarily on the United States and examining the effects of equality on American ideas, mores, and civil society. Significantly, however, an early sketch reflected a quite different and broader design. "Two great divisions: 1. Influence of democracy on ideas; 2. *Id.* on sentiments." He also considered making "a third division of what is not democratic, but American" and wondered where to discuss manners and customs, or "mores properly so-called." Eventually a more definitive plan emerged: "3rd volume. Division to make perhaps. Effects of democracy 1. On thought; 2. On the heart; 3. On habits."[35] Here was an outline that not only revealed a shift away from America, but also captured much of the 1840 *Democracy*, with the notable exception of the fourth great section on the effects of democracy on political society.

By the summer of 1836, Tocqueville realized that he would have to expand the size of the second portion of his work. The scope of his thinking and writing was widening. "Instead of a single volume," he wrote, "I will be *forced* to publish two."[36] Those two volumes of the 1840 *Democracy* would ultimately include four segments, which address, in turn, the influence of democracy on intellectual and cultural life (part 1); on sentiments (part 2); on mores properly so-called (part 3); and on political society (part 4). Parts 1 and 2 would constitute the first volume; parts 3 and 4, the second. As Tocqueville himself realized, America, despite being mentioned in the titles of the first two parts, was fading as the central focus of his book. In a packet of notes, he observed: "The first book [1835] more American than democratic. This one [1840] more democratic than American."[37] As we will see, the 1840 portion would also be even more thoroughly grounded in the French example and pointedly addressed to France. Readers must always remain alert; Tocqueville's book is never all about America.

The 1840 *Democracy* was, in general, shifting not only away from America toward democracy, but also away from the details and specific features of laws and institutions toward more abstract philosophical reflections. Again Tocqueville recognized and worried about this change. Perhaps as a result of this shift toward more deductive and theoretical arguments, his 1840 chapters, often filling only a page or two, grew strikingly shorter than those of 1835; this difference marked a characteristic structural change between the two portions of his book.

For 1840, also in sharp contrast to 1835, Tocqueville's introductory comments were minimal; he provided merely a short preface.[38] But as he drafted his manuscript, he considered writing a more extensive opening, one that would point out to his readers which of his earlier arguments he now considered errors and which had been proved right by recent events in the United States; which of his 1835 opinions he would modify in 1840; and which of his 1840 topics were elaborations on ideas he had already touched upon in 1835.[39] In the end, he opted for brevity.

The second half of *Democracy in America*, in the same two-volume format, finally appeared in April 1840. A year earlier, in 1839, conceding his shift away from America, Tocqueville had temporarily decided to call his last two volumes *The Influence of Equality on the Ideas and Sentiments of Men*. As a sign of important changes in Tocqueville's focus, this con-

sideration of a different title should not be underestimated. But the 1835
work was too famous; Tocqueville found himself almost forced to use the
now familiar title and to publish part 2 of *Democracy in America*.

D ESPITE NOTEWORTHY DIFFERENCES BETWEEN THE SHAPE
of the 1835 and 1840 portions of Tocqueville's work, both halves include clusters of chapters on topics that he considered important. Those
bundles—on, for example, the power of the majority, religion, literature
and the arts, individualism, war and armies, or the family—were not for-
mally separated into discrete parts or sections, but readers should be alert
to how these groupings form distinctive segments of Tocqueville's book.

Before leaving our review of the organization of *Democracy*, we
should also recall how the structure for both the 1835 and 1840 halves of
Tocqueville's work resulted from various choices: to leave some planned
chapters unwritten, to include or delete draft chapters already included in
his manuscript, or to change or retain the order of sections of his book.
His working papers reveal, for example, several chapters planned, but
never completed (on democracy and the moral sciences, on education,
on George Washington, on government support for learned academies);
some others written, but then dropped (on how the Americans act toward corporations, on preaching, on certain tax issues in democracies);
and still others drafted, but almost dropped, saved perhaps by the advice
of others (on how democratic people love equality more than liberty, on
how American democracy has modified the English language, on how
Americans view the equality of the sexes, and on why some Americans
display enthusiastic forms of spirituality). Such choices, made throughout the writing of *Democracy in America*, inevitably influenced the structure and content of Tocqueville's book.

Having examined in broad outline how Tocqueville's *Democracy in
America* took shape—its composition, sources, style of argument, and
organization—we are ready to consider some of the major themes of his
book. In our discussion, we will once again encounter many of Tocqueville's key chapters and even a few of his near chapters.

PART II

WHAT ARE SOME
OF THE MAJOR THEMES
OF TOCQUEVILLE'S
DEMOCRACY?

3

What Are Some of Tocqueville's Basic Convictions?

See in vol. 1 (1835): Tocqueville's introduction, pp. 3–15; part 1, chap. 2, pp. 27–45; part 2, chap. 9, pp. 264–75, 288–98; and chap. 10, pp. 358–59; and in vol. 2 (1840): part 1, chap. 20, pp. 469–72.

THIS CHAPTER INTRODUCES READERS TO THE KEY TOPICS of Tocqueville's *Democracy in America*, not by setting forth a simple catalogue, but by attempting to place Tocqueville's themes within the framework of broader questions about his book, by putting his ideas in context. The difficulties are immense. First, the possible ways to organize the essential themes of *Democracy in America* are many. (We will return to a consideration of some of those possible approaches later.) Second, Tocqueville's ideas are, in some ways, extraordinarily elusive; he never ceased to reconsider his thinking. A mental habit of such ongoing re-examination, of turning and returning (tentative) conclusions, moves Tocqueville's readers along a constantly shifting path, sometimes toward ambiguity and paradox, almost always toward increasing complexity.

Let us begin with what is (relatively) constant, the basic principles of *Democracy in America*. What are some of Tocqueville's most funda-mental convictions? Tocqueville himself talked about his *idées mères*, the beginning concepts that generated and shaped all of his argument. Sev-eral of these *idées mères* (or generative ideas), essential to *Democracy in America*, need to be highlighted.

Tocqueville began his thinking and his book with the fundamen-tal idea that equality of conditions was the defining feature of modern society and that the advance of democracy was inevitable, long-term, and providential. He argued that for centuries equality had been on the march, breaking down all barriers. And he famously asserted that, when he saw what he called the "irresistible [democratic] revolution," he felt "a sort of religious terror" as he contemplated the evidence of God at work in the world.[1]

The coming of a society marked by equality of conditions or democracy meant conversely that the old aristocratic society was disappearing and was inescapably doomed. Aristocracy, based most essentially on landed properties held over generations by the same families, described a society of fixed legal and hereditary castes, where status was largely determined by birth and by laws. Aristocratic society—if it was healthy—featured strong bonds within each family and class and, because of mutual dependency, among all classes. It was marked by social ties, both up and down the social ladder. Aristocracy also implied a society where social, political, and cultural leadership went almost automatically to a small, superior elite. According to Tocqueville, the democratic revolution, at work for seven hundred years, meant the demise of aristocracy, no matter what its presumed advantages might be for social cohesion, political greatness, or cultural brilliance. Aristocracy was gone and could not be brought back.

But Tocqueville argued that the age of equality offered challenges of its own, and he defined the task for his contemporaries (and for all of his readers since) as fostering the benefits and avoiding the pitfalls presented by democracy. His book was in large part a long exercise in teasing out those advantages and disadvantages and suggesting paths for action to enhance the former and avoid the latter. To meet this responsibility of making the best of democracy, he proposed to his readers "a new political science . . . for a world altogether new."[2]

Closely related to Tocqueville's effort to explore the consequences of the democratic revolution was his conviction that no particular political institutions were superior to all others; no constitution was perfect. Ultimately the value of a government depended on how well it fit a given society. Tocqueville declared in an early draft for the introduction of the 1835 *Democracy*: "Governments have relative goodness. When Montesquieu [says that] I admire him. But when he portrays to me the English constitution as the model of perfection, it seems to me that for the first time I see the limits of his genius."[3] In this and other fragments, Tocqueville not only reveals the primary source of one of his bedrock principles, but also explains one reason why, in the pages of his book, he so carefully avoided the trap of portraying American institutions as ideal and as automatically suitable and transferable to other democratic societies.

In *Democracy in America*, Tocqueville began his thinking with the idea of advancing democracy, but perhaps his central concern was how to preserve freedom in the age of equality. Tocqueville spoke for liberty above all else. And he consistently assumed at least a tension, if not an outright contradiction, between equality and liberty. *Democracy in America* was written from the perspective of liberty versus equality. Tocqueville knew that liberty, always fragile, was especially vulnerable in democratic times. (We will examine the multiple meanings of both equality and liberty for Tocqueville in the opening portions of the next chapter.)

Another significant *idée mère* in Tocqueville's book involves the importance of mores (*moeurs*). Tocqueville posited three major causes for the success or failure of any given society: mores, laws, and circumstances. By *mores* he meant the whole moral and intellectual state of a people. "Not only do I apply [the expression]," he wrote, "to *mores* properly so-called, which one could call habits of the heart, but to the different notions that men possess, to the various opinions that are current in their midst, and to the sum of ideas of which the habits of the mind are formed."[4]

No true society, he believed, existed without shared mores. "I shall never agree that men form a society by the sole fact that they recognize the same head and obey the same laws; there is a society only when men consider a great number of objects under the same aspect; when on a great number of subjects they have the same opinions; when, finally, the same facts give rise in them to the same impressions and the same thoughts."[5] Mores also changed slowly and with great difficulty; that too was an essential characteristic.

Laws, for Tocqueville, signified primarily the legal, political, institutional, and constitutional framework and mechanisms created by the makers of fundamental law and by ordinary lawmakers in a society. By *circumstances*, he meant the given historical and physical preconditions or situations in which a society found itself. Most notably, circumstances involved historical origins (or *point of departure*) and physiography, in-

cluding geographic position and environmental resources. In various
parts of the 1835 *Democracy* Tocqueville resorted to the concept of circumstances to help explain why the American republic succeeded.

But as his book took shape, the *point of departure* emerged in his
thinking as probably the most important single circumstance. He would
devote an entire chapter, his second,[6] to the early history of the United
States, stressing the ways in which "antecedent facts" had engendered
American society "as it is organized today."[7] Tocqueville most closely became a historian when he considered the influence of the point of departure on any given society.

Among these three causes, Tocqueville granted primacy to mores. He
insisted that mores—the ideas, beliefs, attitudes, customs, values, and habits particular to each nation—were more crucial to the success or failure
of democracies than laws or circumstances. Mores, he asserted, shaped
societies much more profoundly than legal, or constitutional, or physical, or even economic factors. As Tocqueville understood and presented
them in the pages of his book, mores would be the key to meeting the
challenges posed by democracy. A considerable part of Tocqueville's reputation for creativity and originality as a thinker rests on his sense of the
crucial role played by mores in human society.

While treating such a central concept, Tocqueville characteristically
left several important questions unanswered. His definition remained
conveniently broad and vague. How were mores related to national character, or even to social condition? Mores may be the primary shaper of
society, but what shaped mores? Are mores really so slow to change?
And if they are, how can they be improved? How can beneficial mores
be developed and nurtured in a society? As we move ahead, we will see
other examples of ambiguous definitions, abandoned questions, and unresolved dilemmas.

Still another central principle in Tocqueville's *Democracy* is his fierce
rejection of determinism. Democracy, he argued, is foreordained; increasing equality of condition is inescapable. But the consequences of democracy are not predetermined; neither the benefits nor the dangers are
inevitable. Whether equality arrives with advantages or disadvantages is a
matter of human action and responsibility. Although, as we have already
noted, *Democracy in America* carefully sets forth both democratic dan-

gers and democratic remedies, Tocqueville does not assume that the end result of the democratic revolution is set or known. Instead, he repeatedly declares that democracy could come with either liberty or despotism; the choice is one for the people of each society to make.

It is important to note here that Tocqueville's renunciation of determinism did not allow him to escape entirely from contradiction. The concept of an inescapable (and providential) democratic revolution did not square entirely with his assertion of human choice and freedom of action. Tocqueville realized his problem and resolved in a draft to explain how his system was perfectly compatible with human liberty. Unfortunately, he did not take his own suggestion.

The closest he came in *Democracy in America* to resolving this dilemma about what control nations have over their own destinies appeared in the final few paragraphs of the 1840 portion of his work. "I am not unaware," he wrote,

> that several of my contemporaries have thought that peoples are never masters of themselves here below, and that they necessarily obey I do not know which insurmountable and unintelligent force born of previous events, the race, the soil, or the climate.
>
> Those are false and cowardly doctrines that can never produce any but weak men and pusillanimous nations. Providence has not created the human race either entirely independent or perfectly slave. It traces, it is true, a fatal circle around each man that he cannot leave; but within its vast limits, man is powerful and free; so too with peoples.
>
> Nations of our day cannot have it that conditions within them are not equal; but it depends on them whether equality leads them to servitude or freedom, to enlightenment or barbarism, to prosperity or misery.[8]

As this excerpt reveals, rejecting determinism, for Tocqueville, also meant refusing theories of race and doctrines of materialism. In the early nineteenth century the concept of race was not well defined. In Tocqueville's thinking, for example, it often overlapped with the idea of national character. While he was in America and as he compared the English, French, and German populations of Canada and the United States, he sometimes wrote in his travel diaries about "race" or "blood" as an important cause of observable differences. But by the time he returned to France, he had rejected any idea of racial determinism. The drafts and text of his *Democracy* would consistently reflect his final position.[9]

Tocqueville's refusal to accept determinism, materialism, and racism and his insistence on human freedom and responsibility result from yet another fixed principle: his understanding of the nature of man, a viewpoint heavily influenced by Pascal. Despite his doubts about specific Christian doctrines, Tocqueville believed that the religious impulse is part of human nature, that human beings possess an immortal soul, and that they have a God-given moral responsibility for their choices and actions in the world. Tocqueville had a powerfully expansive concept of human dignity and freedom.

Perhaps one of the best demonstrations of how Tocqueville's beliefs about human responsibility shaped his book occurred in drafts of *Democracy in America*, as he weighed the relative importance of the three causes (mores, laws, and circumstances) mentioned above. As Tocqueville's work developed, his position about the primacy of mores was unchanging. But what about the relative importance of laws and circumstances?

In an initial draft of the chapter from the 1835 portion of his *Democracy* entitled "Of the Principal Causes Tending to Maintain a Democratic Republic in the United States," Tocqueville tentatively concluded:

> Of these three causes the first [circumstances] is the most permanent. . . . Of the three causes the least influential is that of laws and it is, so to speak, the only one that depends on man. . . . People cannot change their position and the original conditions of their existence. A nation can, in the long run, modify its habits and its *moeurs*, but one generation cannot succeed in doing it. It [a single generation] can only change the laws. But, of the three causes about which we are talking, the least influential is precisely that which results from the laws. Not only does man exercise no power over his surroundings, but he possesses, so to speak, none over himself and remains almost completely a stranger to his own fate.[10]

Tocqueville soon realized, however, that this judgment contradicted his belief in human freedom and responsibility. If laws were the least important of the great factors and yet the only one that human beings could readily refashion, what became of human dignity and self-determination? Revisiting the question in another version of his chapter, Tocqueville took his moral convictions into account and reached a very different verdict. "So of the three causes that work together to maintain institutions the least essential is the only one that man cannot create at will [i.e., circumstances], and God, by making their happiness depend particularly on laws and *moeurs*, has in a way placed it in their hands." In a parenthesis, he added: "So physical causes contribute less to the maintenance of institutions than laws; laws, less than *moeurs*."[11] Here, finally, was the ranking that would appear in *Democracy in America*. (And notice how once again what appears in the final text is only the last stage of a long process of reconsideration that led Tocqueville from time to time in quite contrary directions.)

This example of the shifting ranking of the three causes leads us back to Tocqueville the moralist. For him, perhaps the most fundamental issue facing modern human beings was how democracy would influence morality and the "moral sciences." Here, Tocqueville observed, was an "idée capitale et mère." He briefly considered writing a chapter on the subject. "All of man is there," he wrote. Unfortunately, once again he failed to follow his own advice and, after further reflection, decided that the whole topic was "too vast, too thorny."[12] So in his *Democracy*, he never discussed democracy and the moral sciences in any organized way in a single chapter; the topic remained among those specific matters abandoned along the way as *Democracy in America* emerged.

At this point, we see that among the convictions or fundamental principles shaping Tocqueville's book are his thesis about advancing democracy (or equality); his notion that no political institutions are absolutely good; his commitment to liberty; his belief that liberty and equality were a pair in tension; his identification of three causes and his selection of mores as primary among them; his rejection of determinism (including racism and materialism); his elevated vision of human nature and of human freedom and responsibility; and his closely related stance as a moralist who was concerned about the moral implications of democracy. Our consideration of these basic beliefs has also begun to demonstrate in more detail how Tocqueville thought and wrote, and it has begun to reveal the most essential themes and purposes of *Democracy in America*.

4

What Does Tocqueville Mean by
Equality, Democracy, and Liberty?

D EMOCRACY IN AMERICA MAY BE READ AS A BOOK ABOUT "many equalities" and "many democracies." From the beginning, Tocqueville used the terms *equality* and *democracy* somewhat interchangeably. In the opening segments of his book, he presented lists of different types of equality and attempted to offer some clear definitions of democracy (arguably his key concept). But ultimately he failed to settle on any definitive meaning of either *equality* or *democracy*, using the two terms in varied and constantly changing ways and ultimately leaving them ambiguous and imprecise.

EQUALITY

See in vol. 1 (1835): Tocqueville's introduction, especially pp. 3–6; part 1, chap. 3, pp. 45–53; part 2, chap. 2, pp. 170–72. In vol. 2 (1840), see part 3, chap. 5, pp. 546–53; and chap. 13.

As we have already seen, Tocqueville opened his book by focusing on *equality of condition*, the feature of the United States that struck him most vividly. "I discovered without difficulty the enormous influence that [equality of conditions] exerts on the course of society; it gives a certain direction to public spirit, a certain turn to the laws; new maxims to those who govern, and particular habits to the governed."[1] It was a "primary fact," influencing all of political and civil society, including mores; he also called it the "generating fact," source and center of all that he saw in the New World. And he immediately added another important feature. Equality in America was active, in motion, expanding relentlessly toward its extreme limits.

Tocqueville then shifted his attention to Europe and to France. "The same *democracy* reigning in American societies appeared to me to be advancing rapidly toward power in Europe."[2] Note that *equality* had abruptly become *democracy*, and it was on the march everywhere; "a great democratic revolution," he declared, was taking place in both the New and Old Worlds.

In a remarkably brief but eloquent review of seven hundred years of French (and European) history, Tocqueville broadly sketched advancing equality as a "universal leveling" marked by the broadening of access to power in church and state, especially the growing role of clergy and jurists; the fading of political, social, legal, economic, and intellectual hierarchies; the shifting of class status, including the decline of aristocracy and the rise of the middle class; the development of commerce and the creation of new forms of personal wealth that rivaled the traditional influence of landed property; the advance of education and enlightenment; and the discovery of new kinds of knowledge, especially scientific and geographic. For centuries, he asserted, all historical developments seemed both to embody equality and to produce "many new elements of equality," including similar needs, desires, tastes, and passions. Equality was a kind of endlessly self-generating and self-reinforcing fact; it was at once political, social, legal, economic, intellectual, and related to mores.[3]

In the third chapter of the 1835 *Democracy*, entitled "Social State of the Anglo-Americans," Tocqueville returned to equality as it appeared in the New World. He opened the chapter by introducing the concept of the *social state*. "The social state," he wrote, "is ordinarily the product of a fact, sometimes of laws, most often of these two causes united; but once it exists, one can consider it as the first cause of most of the laws, customs and ideas that regulate the conduct of nations; what it does not produce, it modifies."[4]

Note that this definition strikingly parallels Tocqueville's initial description of equality of condition, the essential feature of the American social state. In neither explanation did Tocqueville completely answer the question of what forms or causes, in the first place, either the social state or equality of condition (a particular social state), but he was very firm in his belief that, once established, each becomes the generating force for everything else in society; "what it does not produce, it modifies."

After defining *social state*, Tocqueville then sketched the specific social state he had discovered in the New World, presenting in a few brilliant pages a catalogue of the varieties of equality (among Anglo-Americans) that characterized the United States:

- A broad level of material comfort, a rough equality of property and wealth, and widespread land ownership (*material equality* or *equality of fortunes*). Tocqueville carefully pointed out, however, that equality of fortunes in America did not mean the absence of rich and poor, or any belief in the permanent equality of property.
- The constant circulation of wealth and property, the unceasing rise and fall of individuals and families, and the lack of fixed classes (*equality as mobility*).
- A widely shared basic education and a nearly universal middling level of knowledge (*intellectual equality* or *equality of minds*).
- The disappearance (or at least the fading) of hereditary privilege, rank, and distinction, and the decline of deference (*social equality*). Tocqueville was particularly impressed by the American assumption that everyone had to work and by the American habit of the handshake and the impromptu conversation in the street between shopkeeper and worker, as between equals.
- Fundamentally egalitarian attitudes, ideas, beliefs, religious convictions, habits, and passions, including a deep love of equality (*equality understood in terms of mores*).

For Tocqueville, such a package of equalities had inescapable political consequences, leading to yet another kind of equality. "It is impossible," he declared in his text, "to understand how equality will not in the end penetrate the political world as elsewhere."[5] For the Anglo-Americans, he observed, equality also meant equal political rights (including broad suffrage) and sovereignty of the people (*political equality*).

The catalogue of "many equalities" was not finished, however. Equality also had important psychological dimensions. In the 1840 *Democracy*, Tocqueville would add a pervasive *sentiment of equality*, the sense or feeling that, even in the face of actual inequalities, you are the equal of your fellows and deserve to be treated as such. This sentiment of equality, first noticed by Tocqueville in America, anticipates the later sociological concept of equality of esteem. And it underscores the significance of another feature of an egalitarian society: the sense of fundamental similarity among individuals. In 1840 Tocqueville would note that this working assumption of essential equality not only colored ordinary social encounters, but also shaped the relationship between master and servant and even the bonds among family members.[6]

Both Tocqueville's thumbnail history of advancing equality in France and his more extensive summary of the ways in which Americans were equal point to essentially the same varieties of equality. Arguably, however, the single most significant feature of equality for Tocqueville was relentless movement; equality meant a fluid and open society, a world in motion, where traditional markers of any sort were fixed no longer. In a fragment dated 22 June 1838, he reminded himself: "Explain somewhere what I understand by centuries of equality. It is not that chimerical time when all men are perfectly similar and equal, but those (1) . . . when a greater number [of men] will fall either above or below, but not far from the common measure; (2) . . . when there will be no more permanent classification, caste, class, any insurmountable barrier, or even one very difficult to surmount; so that if all men are not equal, they can all aspire to the same point."[7]

Some readers have misunderstood what equality meant for Tocqueville and have misconstrued his assertions about American equality in particular. We need to remember that Tocqueville always recognized the existence of classes and of rich and poor in democratic societies, and as we will see more clearly later, he acknowledged various other inequalities that existed in the United States. For him, equality evoked, among other things, social and economic mobility, not social and economic sameness.

Here we need to acknowledge what Tocqueville ranked as one of the primary causes of the broad and advancing equality that he had witnessed in the United States. He pointed to inheritance laws that forbid primogeniture and entail, thereby favoring the division of the landholdings of each successive generation, and undermining any possibility of maintaining a traditional aristocracy. Tocqueville believed that changes in inheritance laws, after the American Revolution in the New World republic, and during the early nineteenth century in France, were one of the fundamental reasons for the ongoing democratic revolution. "I am astonished," he declared, "that ancient and modern political writers have not attributed to estate laws a greater influence on the course of human affairs. These laws belong, it is true, to the civil order; but they ought to be placed at the head of all political institutions, for they have an incredible influence on the social state of peoples, of which political laws are only the expression."[8] This idea, often criticized as exaggerated and even as something of a personal fixation, is nonetheless part of the argument of his book.

DEMOCRACY

See in vol. 1 (1835): Tocqueville's introduction, esp. pp. 7–12; part 1, chaps. 3 and 4; and part 2, chap. 6, pp. 231–35; and chap. 9, pp. 298–302.

Equality, in all its guises, defined the social state of the Anglo-Americans, which was, according to Tocqueville, "eminently democratic." But what did he mean by *democracy*? Were *equality of condition* and *democracy* entirely the same thing? Tocqueville went back and forth in his answer. "As soon as you look at the civil and political society of the United States, you discover two great facts that dominate all the others and from which the others are derived. *Democracy constitutes the social state*; the dogma of the sovereignty of the people, the political law. These two things are not analogous. *Democracy is society's way of being*; sovereignty of the people, a form of government." But in the margin he reminded himself: "Note that . . . the social state must never be confused with the political laws that follow from it; equality or inequality of conditions, which are facts, with democracy or aristocracy, which are laws. Reexamine from this point of view."[9] Was democracy a specific social state, or particular political laws?

Tocqueville never gave a definitive answer. Some of his definitions of democracy, despite his reminders to himself, continued to focus on social state or civil society and closely mirrored or even repeated his definitions of equality. Democracy was a particular social state marked by equality of conditions and made manifest in the United States. It was a brute fact, a universal leveling, an irreversible current, a rising flood, an immense social revolution. Especially as Tocqueville drafted the 1840 *Democracy*, he tended to conflate equality and democracy and, as many trial titles of chapters in his working manuscript testify, to use the two terms interchangeably.

As he wrote, he realized that his treatment of democracy as equality was often exaggerated, highly abstract, and perhaps dangerously removed from real examples. In order to be well understood, he found himself constantly obliged to depict extreme states, an aristocracy without a mixture of democracy, or a democracy without a mixture of aristocracy. Entirely theoretical portraits of aristocracy or democracy were nonetheless useful intellectual tools for Tocqueville. They clarified his argument for his readers and helped him to compare and contrast salient features of differing social states. And once again, his ways of thinking anticipated later developments in political and social theory. His *extreme states* foreshadowed the *ideal types* of modern political scientists.

But democracy, in social terms, went beyond the many specific equalities listed by Tocqueville, or *equality of condition* as a theoretical abstraction. When Tocqueville wrote the word *democracy* in his drafts and working manuscript, he sometimes had particular classes in mind. At times *(the) democracy* meant the people, usually implying the lower classes, but occasionally signifying the entire people, as in the phrase "sovereignty of the people." At other times he identified the democratic class par excellence as the middle class. Democracy, he sometimes asserted, meant the dominating influence throughout society of the middle classes. And at least once in his drafts, he described (the) democracy as the "industrial class," the owners of industry, a particular slice of the middle class.[10]

The sense of democracy as the people (or as the lower classes) clarifies one of the most frequently repeated pleas in Tocqueville's book: "I wish that the upper classes and the middle classes of all of Europe were as persuaded as I am myself that henceforth it is no longer a matter of knowing if the people will attain power, but in what manner they will use their power. That is the great problem of the future. . . . The great, the capital interest of the century is the organization and the education of [the] democracy."[11] In his text, he observed: "The most powerful, most intelligent and most moral classes of the nation have not sought to take hold of it [the democracy] so as to direct it. Democracy has therefore been abandoned to its savage instincts; it has grown up like those children who, deprived of paternal care, rear themselves in the streets of our towns and know only society's vices and miseries."[12]

Tocqueville never abandoned his understanding of democracy as a social state or social classes, but democracy, like equality, had a political as well as a social dimension. Tocqueville began to broaden his definition of democracy to include explicitly political meanings. Democracy meant particular political laws. Democracy, "properly so-called" Tocqueville wrote in one draft, signified the dogma of the sovereignty of the people and the principle of the majority (majority rule). In another fragment, he equated democracy with equal political rights for all citizens. And in yet another draft, he declared that whenever the government of a people is the sincere and permanent expression of the will of the greatest number, the government whatever its form, is democratic. So democracy in its political dimension included sovereignty of the people, majority rule, equal political rights (including broad suffrage), widespread participation in public affairs, and a government based on the (true) will of the people. Note that democracy for Tocqueville did not require a republican form of government.[13]

Understanding the two facets of democracy—social and political, that is, social state and political laws—is essential for grasping Tocqueville's thinking. The dual dimensions of democracy were intimately linked; and for Tocqueville the balance or harmony between the two was crucial.

In the introduction to the 1835 *Democracy*, Tocqueville portrayed three distinct societies as types: an idealized France of the old regime before its decay, the model of aristocratic society at its best, marked by "stability, power and above all glory"; France of the early nineteenth century, a society torn apart and out of joint; and the model of a healthy democratic society, largely patterned on the American republic (also idealized).[14] Tocqueville's description of contemporary France presents a society caught between two worlds and in a "strange confusion." "I find nothing that should evoke more sadness and more pity than what is passing before our eyes."[15] Strikingly different was his picture of the well-ordered American republic, which seemed to have found ways to make democracy highly beneficial to society. How to explain this painful contrast between a diseased and a healthy democracy? How best to heal France? (Here perhaps was Tocqueville's most fundamental question and the most basic reason for his book.)

A close examination of Tocqueville's portraits reveals that, for him, the relationship between social and political democracy provides the key to an answer. France since the Revolution (and even long before) had experienced at least some measure of democracy in the social realm; but democracy in terms of politics was stillborn. Social democracy (or civil society) was out of joint with political democracy (or political society). The American republic, on the other hand, was a society where, from the beginning, both social and political democracy had flourished in tandem. French society was fractured and at war with itself because political democracy lagged behind an existing social democracy. American society was healthy because the two facets of democracy—social and political—were in harmony.

Another way to understand this argument is to recall Tocqueville's discussion of mores and laws. His point about the need for harmony between the social and political dimensions of democracy reflects his belief that, for a society to function well, laws need to be appropriate to mores. For Tocqueville, a mismatch between democracy as political laws and democracy as social state, or between laws and mores, is destructive for any nation or people.

As we have already seen, Tocqueville argued that, in the age of democracy, whatever the attractions, benefits, and charms of aristocracy may have been, they are gone irretrievably. So the challenge that Tocqueville posed for his readers is not somehow to revive aristocracy (a fool's errand), but to discern the best and worst possibilities of democracy and to learn to promote the first while avoiding the second. Matching political laws to social state, political democracy to social democracy, was one of the first lessons for achieving this goal. To cure democracy (social), you needed more democracy (political).

We also need to recognize here, parenthetically and in passing, that Tocqueville's depictions of nineteenth-century France and America touch on another key reason for the differences between the two societies. France had suffered a violent revolution; the United States, according to Tocqueville, was born without a revolution. (His rather dismissive judgment about the American Revolution remains one of his more notable errors.) Especially in the 1840 portion of his book, the negative impact of revolution and of what Tocqueville came to call the "revolutionary spirit" would become far more important to him, and he would struggle to separate what was democratic from what was revolutionary in his analysis of democratic societies (especially France). We will come back to this point later.

LIBERTY

See in vol. 1 (1835): part 1, chaps. 2 and 3, esp. pp. 52–53; and part 2, chap. 9, pp. 298–302; and in vol. 2 (1840): part 2, chaps. 4 and 5; and part 4, chap. 7.

Tocqueville's personal passion for liberty has already been noted; the supreme value of freedom was one of his absolute convictions. In his 1835 introduction he referred to "the holy cult of freedom."[16] And from the opening pages, his *Democracy* may be read largely as a defense of liberty against the potential assaults of an egalitarian age. But his use of the word *liberty* was no exception to Tocqueville's habit of using key words in multiple ways.

The term had several meanings for him. Most profoundly, he assumed a moral liberty. His book was written with the belief that human beings were free and independent agents ultimately responsible for their choices and actions. Tocqueville also assumed what may be called historical liberty. Although he was no philosopher of history and remained chronically vague about the fundamental cause (or causes) that drove history, and although he argued that advancing democracy was inescapable, he absolutely rejected any sort of historical determinism, as we have already seen; he always presumed a substantial circle of freedom in which human beings could work out their own historical destiny.

In the second chapter of the 1835 *Democracy*, on the American point of departure, Tocqueville introduced still other kinds of liberty. While sketching the remarkable social and political democracy of the Puritans, he quoted at length from the famous speech given in 1645 by John Winthrop, perennial governor of the Massachusetts Bay Colony, in which Winthrop distinguished between *natural liberty* and *civil liberty*. Natural liberty referred to liberty in a corrupt or fallen nature, when men were free to do whatever they pleased. Civil liberty meant freedom hedged in by moral constraints and by the community good, liberty within the confines of religious belief and legal and constitutional agreements.

Tocqueville declared Winthrop's remarks a "beautiful definition of freedom."[17] He agreed that true human freedom existed within God-given bounds of morality and justice and needed to be exercised within the context of public life; liberty, to be full or complete, required involvement in the shared life of the community or society. Tocqueville continued: "I have already said enough to put . . . Anglo-American civilization in its true light. It is the product (and this point of departure ought constantly to be present in one's thinking) of two perfectly distinct elements that elsewhere have often made war with each other, but which, in America, they have succeeded in incorporating somehow into one another and combining marvelously. I mean to speak of the *spirit of religion* and the *spirit of freedom*."[18] Here was still another dimension of liberty: the spirit of freedom.

Yet another way for Tocqueville to define liberty was to move beyond the abstract concept and focus on particular liberties. First of all, liberties meant certain legal, constitutional, and institutional mechanisms that a society or people could establish to promote freedom. Use of such devices was one of the characteristics that Tocqueville admired most about the Americans. They had attempted to spread or scatter power in their republic by setting up particular institutional and legal arrangements, including local liberties, associations, juries, the federal system, checks and balances among the branches of government (including bicameralism and an independent and active judiciary), liberty of the press, and individual civil and political rights (such as freedom of speech and the rights to assemble and to vote).

As Tocqueville wrote in the 1840 *Democracy*:

> It is therefore above all in the democratic times we are in that the true friends of freedom and human greatness must constantly remain on their feet and ready to prevent the social power from lightly sacrificing the particular rights of some individuals to the general execution of its designs. In these times there is no citizen so obscure that it is not very dangerous to allow him to be oppressed, nor are there individual rights of so little importance that one can deliver them with impunity to arbitrariness. . . . To violate [the particular right of an individual] in our day is to corrupt national mores profoundly and to put society as a whole in peril. . . .[19]

For Tocqueville, *liberty* without *liberties* was empty of meaning.

The particular liberties and the key legal and structural mechanisms that Tocqueville observed in the United States provided some of the most important specific lessons that he would offer in his book. With the significant exception of federalism, which he felt was inappropriate to the exposed geographic position of France, those liberties and devices became essential parts of the political program that he faithfully set forth in both the 1835 and 1840 parts of *Democracy in America*.

Liberties, for Tocqueville, also evoked certain ingrained ideas, behaviors, habits, and values, such as the spirit of locality, the spirit of association, the spirit of religion, practical political experience, public and private morality, a sense of justice, respect for law, public spirit, sensitivity to the rights of others, a grasp of how private and public interest could be blended effectively, and general enlightenment. "In order for democracy to govern," he wrote in one of his drafts, "citizens are needed who take an interest in public affairs, who *have the capacity* to get involved and who *want* to do so. Capital point to which one must always return."[20]

Tocqueville sometimes referred to the specific mechanisms as involving the *art of liberty*, and to the attitudes, ideas and behaviors as reflecting the *habits* (or *spirit*) *of liberty*. The art of liberty meant primarily the work of constitution makers and legislators; it was to a large degree manmade, relying on sound principles and knowledge about how to organize, facilitate, and sustain certain legal and institutional arrangements. The habits (or spirit) of liberty arose not from the work of legislators, but from a long history of inherited attitudes and behaviors; they emerged over time.

Once again, Tocqueville's analysis echoes his fundamental distinction between laws and mores. Liberties as devices (institutions and rights) are closely related to laws; liberties as habits, to mores. And, as we might expect, just as mores are more important than laws, Tocqueville argued that the habits of liberty are more powerful and enduring, more essential and reliable in a given society than the art of liberty. A nation that enjoys the first can tolerate bad laws; this, to a degree, was how Tocqueville saw the American republic.[21] A nation that relies on the art of liberty to shape favorable habits faces long and difficult work; this, from Tocqueville's perspective, was the challenge facing France in the early nineteenth century. Note, however, that the art of liberty is useful and even necessary, especially if the habits of liberty are weak or absent. Laws matter, and they can be used to shape mores in the long term.

So Tocqueville spoke not only for freedom or liberty in the abstract, but also for *liberties*, including a specific list of political and civil rights. More broadly, he envisioned liberties as the keys to civic involvement and the broadest possible public participation.[22] Liberties—as art and habits—were essential to his understanding of citizenship and public life. First of all, they provided a *passive* framework. To be a free citizen, you need a voice. So Tocqueville stressed wider suffrage (at least in the pages of his *Democracy*); local self-government (what he called local liberties); the fundamental rights to write, speak, associate and assemble; freedom of the press; the jury system; a strong, independent judiciary; and separation of church and state. These fundamental freedoms and preconditions open the door to genuine citizenship; they make public participation possible.

But the primary dimension of liberty for Tocqueville was *active*. True freedom meant public participation, especially at the local level, through localities (or towns) and associations; it involved what Tocqueville called the *spirit of locality* (or town spirit) and the spirit of association. Ongoing, day-to-day involvement in public affairs fostered the habits of liberty. Liberty, as active participation, also assumed a strong sense of individual moral responsibility for what happens in the wider society. Here, in genuine civic involvement, was the heart of what Tocqueville understood by liberty. This close linkage of liberty and participation sets Tocqueville sharply apart from other French political writers of his time; it is one of the distinguishing marks of his originality as a theorist.

Tocqueville's sense of liberties, as art and habits, and of the passive and active facets of freedom resemble later notions of *positive* and *negative* liberty—a rough parallel that is very useful for grasping the complexity of Tocqueville's definition of liberty. Negative liberty provides specific rights or freedoms—for example, the right to vote, the liberty to associate, or freedom of the press. Positive liberty goes beyond the simple provision of a right. Just as the *habits* of liberty give life to the *art* of liberty, positive liberty assures that rights granted are not empty of substance. Freedom of the press is meaningless without widespread literacy or the existence of competing publications. The right to vote is useless if there is no opposition able to organize and express its views freely, or if you are turned away by force from the polling place (as Tocqueville knew happened to free blacks in some of the northern states of America). The liberty to associate is hollow if those seeking to assemble are denied meeting places, physically threatened as they gather, or prevented from expressing their dissenting views. Positive liberty entails the capacity for genuine political participation. It echoes Tocqueville's own profound understanding of what real freedom meant.

HOW ARE EQUALITY, DEMOCRACY, AND LIBERTY RELATED?

See in vol. 1 (1835): part 1, chap. 3, pp. 52–53; and in vol. 2 (1840): part 2, chaps. 1 and 13; and part 4, chap. 1.

As we have seen, Tocqueville, despite self-reminders, never escaped his tendency to use the terms *democracy* and *equality* interchangeably; the "many democracies" he described closely paralleled the "many equalities." Especially in its social dimension, democracy most fundamentally meant equality of condition. So for Tocqueville, the hallmark of democracy was equality.

Democracy was emphatically not synonymous with liberty, however. As we have already noted, *Democracy in America* is, in large part, an exploration of how best to preserve liberty in the face of advancing democracy. For Tocqueville, equality and liberty, far from being companions, are at odds; democracy, understood as equality, put freedom at risk. American readers need to be especially wary here because they commonly use the term *democracy* rather vaguely and reflexively as meaning both equality and liberty. Tocqueville did not make this mistake. He easily imagined, for example, a society of equals living under the absolute rule of one man who alone stood above the crowd (democracy without liberty).

Nonetheless, when he considered the psychological effects of democracy, he noticed that democracy produced two distinct passions: one for equality and one for liberty; and the first was far stronger than the second. In the 1835 portion of his book he observed: "Peoples whose social state is democratic . . . have an instinctive taste for [liberty]. But freedom is not the principal and continuous object of their desire; what they love with an eternal love is equality; they dash toward freedom with a rapid impulse and sudden efforts, and if they miss the goal, they resign themselves; but nothing can satisfy them without equality, and they would sooner consent to perish than to lose it."[23]

In one of his most famous chapters, "Why Democratic Peoples Show a More Ardent and More Lasting Love for Equality Than for Freedom," found in the 1840 *Democracy*, Tocqueville elaborated on this argument. "The taste that men have for freedom and the one they feel for equality are in fact two distinct things, and I do not fear to add that among democratic peoples they are two unequal things."[24] In this chapter he presented several reasons for the democratic preference for equality (over liberty) and concluded: "I think that democratic peoples have a natural taste for freedom; left to themselves they seek it, they love it, and they will see themselves parted from it only with sorrow. But for equality they have an ardent, insatiable, eternal, invincible passion; they want equality in freedom, and, if they cannot get it, they still want it in slavery."[25]

So democratic peoples want equality above all else and are willing to trade freedom for equality if necessary. Democracy, as equality of condition, could come with either despotism or liberty. Here is another one of the central arguments of Tocqueville's book.

Tocqueville's consideration of the passion for equality led him to other, sometimes quite counterintuitive, insights as well. In the 1835 *Democracy*, he noted that the desire for equality could never be satisfied. "Democratic institutions awaken and flatter the passion for equality without ever being able to satisfy it entirely. Every day this complete equality eludes the hands of the people at the moment when they believe they have seized it, and it flees, as Pascal said, in an eternal flight."[26] He would develop this idea further in the 1840 text, noting first that perfect and complete equality was impossible, and second that while equality opened the road to all, it also led to inevitable crowding and blocked ambitions.[27] So people in democracies were left always striving for what was unattainable and always unsatisfied. Behind this frustration, Tocqueville saw a remarkable paradox. He realized that dissatisfaction and envy in egalitarian societies increase as actual inequalities diminish. As people become more equal to their fellows, any relatively small, remaining inequalities become even more irritating and intolerable.[28] With *equality of condition*, perennial frustration is the human condition.

Tocqueville also kept returning to the love of liberty engendered by democracy. In the 1840 part of his book, he again expanded upon ideas he had broached in 1835, and described how men who live in democratic times have a taste for free institutions and lean instinctively toward political independence.[29] Although these democratic effects are overshadowed by the strength of the passion for equality, they deserve, nonetheless, to be emphasized. Some readers of Tocqueville's work focus perhaps too much on the dangers of democracy and on the threat that the passion for equality, pushed to the point of delirium,[30] poses for freedom; they tend to miss the positive links between democracy and liberty that Tocqueville described and forget that democracy also gives birth to a love of liberty, a taste for free institutions, and a propensity for political independence.

What can we conclude at this point? Our review of Tocqueville's consideration of equality, democracy, and liberty demonstrates the importance of certain initial sections of his *Democracy*, especially the introduction and the opening chapters of the 1835 portion. These segments—announcements, in a sense, of all that would follow—are essential to any exposition of his ideas. We have seen more than once that, at the beginning of his work, Tocqueville introduced major themes that he would develop in the course of the 1835 *Democracy* and even beyond in the 1840 text, whether his observation that democracy fostered passions for both equality and liberty, his realization that the desire for equality was stronger than the love of liberty, his insight that equality always slipped beyond reach and ultimately left human beings frustrated, envious, and unsatisfied, or his recognition of the problem of distinguishing between what was democratic and what was revolutionary. In each case, the initial mention in 1835 foreshadowed further discussion either later in the 1835 portion or in 1840.

We have also noted that Tocqueville's ways of thinking and writing sometimes anticipated future social scientific approaches. His extreme states, for example, remind us of ideal types; his understanding of the sentiment of equality parallels the modern concept of equality of esteem; and his sense of the passive and active facets of liberty reminds us of the notion of negative and positive liberty. As we move ahead, we will discover other examples of this talent for foreshadowing later theoretical ideas and methods.

Our survey has also revealed some of the basic purposes of Tocqueville's book. We can already acknowledge his effort to show how the social and political ills of nineteenth-century France could be cured; his message that the outcome of democracy (liberty or despotism) depended on our actions; and his presentation of proposals for how best to defend liberty in the age of democracy.

Finally, we have discussed Tocqueville's understanding of how laws and mores shape society and his belief that the latter were always more fundamental than the former. And we have seen how his analysis of laws and mores as causes influenced his views about the need for harmony between the social and political dimensions of democracy and about the relative importance of the art and habits of liberty. His initial analysis of three causes—circumstances, laws, and mores—would cast a long shadow throughout his *Democracy*.

5

How Does Democracy
Threaten Liberty?

THREE PARTICULAR DEMOCRATIC THREATS TO LIBERTY especially worried Tocqueville: materialism, individualism, and centralization. The story of how his understanding of these three dangers developed is not straightforward; it involves some remarkable new insights and shifts of emphasis by Tocqueville. And, as we will observe, Tocqueville often found America exempt from his worst fears.

DEMOCRATIC MATERIALISM

See in vol. 1 (1835): part 2, chap. 9, pp. 265–74; and chap. 10, pp. 384–90; and in vol. 2 (1840): part 2, chaps. 10, 11, 14, and 15.

Tocqueville's intellectual exploration of democratic materialism began in America. Within days of his arrival in the New World, in his travel notebooks and letters home, he began to develop a description of the American national character. One trait emerged almost immediately; the Americans were strikingly materialistic. In an early letter home, Tocqueville remarked: "The whole world here seems a malleable material that man turns and fashions to his liking. . . . Nothing is easier than becoming rich in America; naturally, the human spirit, which needs a dominant passion, in the end turns all its thoughts toward gain. As a result, at first sight this people seems to be a company of merchants joined together for trade, and as one digs deeper into the national character of the Americans, one sees that they have sought the value of everything in this world only in the answer to this single question: how much money will it bring in?"[1]

Similar comments recur repeatedly in Tocqueville's travel diaries where he mentions the "greed for wealth," "the thirst for gain," and "the commercial fervor which seems to devour the whole of society." In a brief discussion of American morality and hard work, he declared: "If the number of human passions seems restricted here, it is because they have all been absorbed in just one: the love of wealth."[2]

Tocqueville carried these ideas directly into the 1835 *Democracy*, where he described the immoderate desire for wealth of the Americans and wrote:

> The American republics [or states] in our day are like companies of merchants, formed to exploit in common the wilderness lands of the New World, and busy in a commerce that is prospering. The passions that agitate the Americans most profoundly are commercial passions and not political passions, or rather, they carry the habits of trade into politics. They love order, without which affairs cannot prosper, and they particularly prize regularity of mores, on which good houses [of business] are founded; they prefer the good sense that creates great fortunes to the genius that often dissipates them; general ideas frighten their minds, accustomed to positive calculations, and among them [the Americans], practice is more in honor than theory.[3]

(Note how the 1835 mention of the American dislike of general ideas and preference for practice above theory anticipates the fuller discussion in the early chapters of the first part of the 1840 *Democracy*.)[4]

We should also acknowledge briefly here that Tocqueville's treatment of the American mercantile impulse was not entirely negative. When, in the 1835 *Democracy*, he considered the future commercial greatness of the United States, he would lavish praise on the American spirit of enterprise.[5] But his concern about excessive materialism remained.

After 1835, as Tocqueville drafted the second part of his book, the American pursuit of the comforts of life was transformed in his thinking into a general democratic characteristic. By 1840, brief passages about democratic materialism would appear in various places in his book, and he would ultimately devote two separate small chapters specifically to the passion for material well-being.[6] In those chapters, Tocqueville would ar-

gue explicitly that the materialism he had witnessed in America marked
other democratic societies as well; the trait was not American, but democratic in nature.

How to explain this new emphasis? Perhaps his journeys to England
in 1833 and 1835 focused his attention on the way in which American behavior reflected the materialism of the English middle class. Or perhaps,
by the late 1830s, Tocqueville was becoming more personally troubled
by what he saw as the increasing materialism of the society around him.
Certainly, he began to recognize the various ways in which growing materialism could threaten liberty. In any case, the concept of democratic
materialism is an important example of an idea that, for Tocqueville, first
emerged in America, briefly appeared in the 1835 text, and then took on
far greater importance in the second part of his *Democracy*.

"In America," Tocqueville wrote in 1840, "the passion for material
well-being is . . . general. . . . The care of satisfying the least needs of the
body and of providing the smallest comforts of life preoccupies minds
universally. Something like this is more and more to be seen in Europe."
In democratic societies, he added, "[people] apply themselves constantly
to pursuing or keeping these enjoyments that are so precious, so incom-
plete, and so fleeting."[7]

This all-consuming democratic passion for well-being had several
potentially dangerous results. First, it produced a preference for order.
Tocqueville pointed out to his readers that the love of wealth and material
enjoyments, which was often suspect in Europe as a cause of shocking
excesses and social disorder, pushed democratic peoples instead toward
moderation and stability. To attain and keep the comforts of life, order
and predictability were necessary.

Here, as in other cases, the Americans, with their commercial habits
and well-regulated mores, served as the example. By 1840, he insisted that
this link between the love of well-being and the need for order was, once
again, not simply American, but democratic. And the preference for order, as we will soon see, opened the door to possible despotism. Here was
the first way that democratic materialism threatened liberty.

A second negative result of materialistic desires was moral decay. In
his 1840 chapters about the love of well-being, Tocqueville described the
potentially dangerous moral consequences of this democratic passion.

The Americans, he recalled, balanced the pursuit of wealth and physical enjoyments with deep religious faith; earthly desires were limited by religion. This counterbalance did not exist in other democracies, where materialistic passions threatened to have quite opposite moral results. "What I reproach equality for," Tocqueville summarized in the 1840 text, "is not that it carries men away in the pursuit of forbidden enjoyments; it is for absorbing them entirely in the search for permitted enjoyments. Thus there could well be established in the world a sort of honest materialism that does not corrupt souls, but softens them and in the end quietly loosens all their tensions."[8]

What did he mean? In part his message was religious or spiritual. He lamented a retreat from spiritual striving in favor of material gains and a reluctance to engage in any efforts that promised no physical rewards. He worried that democratic peoples would lose sight of higher, nonmaterial goals. Here was the moral challenge of the desire for well-being.

But hidden in this loosening of tensions was the third dangerous result of democratic materialism: the relaxation of the springs of action. Tocqueville was worried about liberty as public participation. The pursuit of wealth and material well-being diverted energy from anything other than private gain and private comfort. Here, once again, Tocqueville realized that the American case was exceptional. The New World republicans lived not only with religion that moderated materialistic desires, but also with particular laws and institutions that strongly encouraged public participation, and they possessed both a love of liberty and a highly sophisticated understanding of how private and public interests could merge and reinforce each other.[9] Elsewhere, in societies lacking these characteristics, the drive toward well-being discouraged involvement in public affairs and led to a decline in civic involvement. Materialism drove democratic peoples (other than the Americans) toward an exclusive concern for private well-being. Such a refusal to spend time on public affairs, as well as an insistence on order above all else, led toward despotism.

In the 1840 portion of his book, Tocqueville warned:

There is, in fact, a very perilous passage in the life of democratic peoples. When the taste for material enjoyments develops in one of these peoples more rapidly than enlightenment and the habits of freedom, there comes a moment when men are swept away and almost beside themselves at the sight of the new goods that they are ready to grasp. Preoccupied with the sole care of making a fortune, they no longer perceive the tight bond that unites the particular fortune of each of them to the prosperity of all. . . . If, at this critical moment, an ambitious, able man comes to take possession of power, he finds the way open to every usurpation. . . .

I shall acknowledge without difficulty that public peace is a great good; but I nevertheless do not want to forget that it is through good order that all peoples have arrived at tyranny. . . . A nation that demands of its government only the maintenance of order is already a slave at the bottom of its heart; it is a slave to its well-being, and the man who is to put it in chains can appear. The despotism of factions is no less to be dreaded there than that of one man. When the mass of citizens wants to be occupied only with private affairs, the smallest parties should not despair of becoming masters of public affairs.[10]

So the demand for order and the avoidance of public activity that could arise from the democratic desire for well-being opened the door to tyranny, exercised either by one man or by a faction. Here were two of the many faces of despotism that Tocqueville would present in the two parts of his *Democracy*.

In 1831, when Tocqueville began to consider the problem of materialistic mores, America first served as the illustration of a society consumed by the love of money and the pursuit of well-being. As he wrote the 1840 portion of his book, however, the New World republic became more of an exception than an example. Americans could not escape democratic materialism, but they were insulated from its most dangerous consequences by their religious faith, love of liberty, habits of public participation, and understanding of how private and public interests were linked. Readers of Tocqueville's *Democracy* need always to be vigilant about how, at any given point in his thinking and writing, America fits into his argument.

We have already noted that, largely on moral grounds, Tocqueville rejected and condemned materialism as a philosophical doctrine. Now we see that he also worried about the materialistic mores that, according to his analysis, marked democratic societies. He argued that democratic materialism risked an exaggerated preference for order, a morally unhealthy focus on worldly enjoyments, and a shortsighted reluctance to give time and energy to public, rather than private matters. These tendencies came from the desire for well-being, and each one was dangerous for liberty.

DEMOCRATIC INDIVIDUALISM

See in vol. 1 (1835): part 2, chap. 6, pp. 231–35; and in vol. 2 (1840): part 2, chaps. 2–4 and 8.

In the 1840 *Democracy*, Tocqueville presented democratic materialism and democratic individualism as a pair, devoting several adjoining chapters to each concept. Tocqueville's use of the word *individualism* is, in itself, noteworthy. Although the term had first appeared in France in the early 1820s, its use was still rare enough, even in 1840, for Tocqueville to point out that "*individualism* is a recent expression arising from a new idea. Our fathers knew only selfishness [egoism]."[11] Strictly speaking, the term was not what Tocqueville often sought, a new word to describe novel things. But if the expression was not entirely new to the French, Tocqueville's 1840 book did introduce the word *individualism* to the English language.

What did Tocqueville mean by individualism? In the working papers and text of the 1835 portion, he had written repeatedly about egoism (or selfishness). One draft of the 1840 *Democracy* continued that habit: "*Egoism. How democracy tends to develop the egoism natural to the human heart. When conditions are equal, when each person is more or less sufficient unto himself and has neither the duty to give nor to receive from anyone else, it is natural that he withdraws into himself and that for him society ends where his family ends.*"[12] In the 1840 text, however, he carefully distinguished between egoism, a traditional and familiar narcissism or selfishness, and individualism, the result of democracy.

Selfishness is a passionate and exaggerated love of self that brings man to relate everything to himself alone and to prefer himself to everything.

Individualism is a reflective and peaceable sentiment that disposes each citizen to isolate himself from the mass of those like him and to withdraw to one side with his family and his friends, so that, after having thus created a little society for his own use, he willingly abandons society at large to itself.

Selfishness is born of a blind instinct; individualism proceeds from an erroneous judgment rather than a depraved sentiment. It has its source in the defects of the mind as much as in the vices of the heart.

Selfishness withers the seed of all the virtues; individualism at first dries up only the source of public virtues; but in the long run it attacks and destroys all the others and will finally be absorbed in selfishness.

Selfishness is a vice as old as the world. It scarcely belongs more to one form of society than to another.

Individualism is of democratic origin, and it threatens to develop as conditions become equal.[13]

In his chapter Tocqueville explained once again how democracy loosens the ties between classes and even those linking one generation to another. And he argued that democratic individualism involved not simply "vices of the heart," but "defects of the mind." To a large degree, individuals in democratic times *decided* to withdraw into a small circle of family and friends and leave the wider world to itself; Tocqueville called this decision an "erroneous judgment." He believed that those who succumbed to democratic individualism failed to understand that what happened in the larger society would ultimately influence their private existence; a radical separation of private and public realms was not possible.

American readers of Tocqueville's work, especially, need to recognize from the outset that his concept of individualism differs from theirs. He consistently used the word in a pejorative way. For him, it signified a corrosive sort of excessive privatism that saps civic virtue and weakens public life; it turns people away from common interests and toward narrow private concerns. In contrast, for most Americans, individualism evokes positive characteristics, including self-reliance, a kind of tough independence, and a sense of individual responsibility. This was not what Tocqueville meant by the term in his *Democracy*.

The sense of individualism as one of the negative consequences of democracy was not entirely new for Tocqueville in 1840. In drafts for the first part of his book, he lamented that when people were excluded from public participation, they became indifferent to their interests and enemies of their own rights; they might be called peaceful inhabitants or good family men, but they were emphatically not citizens. Such men did not initially stand apart from civic life by choice, but the individual's isolation and noninvolvement paralleled what Tocqueville would later call *individualism*. And in the 1835 text Tocqueville got even closer to his 1840 idea. "In certain countries, the inhabitant only accepts with a sort of repugnance the political rights that the law accords him; it seems that to occupy him with common interests is to steal his time, and he likes to enclose himself in a narrow selfishness of which four ditches topped by a hedge form the exact limits."[14] Here the "good family man" himself chose not to get involved in common interests; he happily limited himself instead to his own small private world.

Tocqueville's concept of individualism as it emerged during the 1830s also serves as a good example of how the behavior of certain people around him helped to shape the writing of his *Democracy*. In the 1830s, at least two of his closest friends, Louis de Kergorlay and Eugène Stoffels (brother of Charles Stoffels), joined many others of their countrymen in a kind of internal exile. Out of political frustration, or disgust, or disillusionment they made a considered judgment to withdraw from any public involvement and to concentrate their energies and talents on family and private concerns. This turning inward deeply troubled Tocqueville as both a lamentable waste and a terrible sickness of the times.

In 1838, Tocqueville complained to Pierre Paul Royer-Collard, political figure and mentor to Tocqueville, about the incessant intrusions and demands of his Norman neighbors.

I am attached to this population, without, all the same, concealing its faults which are great. These people here are honest, intelligent, religious enough, passably moral, very steady; but they have scarcely any disinterestedness. It is true that egoism in this region does not resemble that of Paris, so violent and often so cruel. It is a mild, calm, and tenacious love of private interests,

which bit by bit absorbs all other sentiments of the heart and dries up
almost all sources of enthusiasm there. They join to this egoism a certain
number of private virtues and domestic qualities which, as a whole, form
respectable men and poor citizens.

The reply from Royer-Collard was sharp: "You are peeved about the
country where you live; but your *Normans*, they are France, they are the
world; this prudent and intelligent egoism, it is the *honnêtes gens* [good
or decent people] of our time, trait for trait."[15] To a remarkable degree,
what Tocqueville observed among his friends and neighbors matched the
description of democratic individualism that would appear in 1840.

Tocqueville's fears about rampant individualism put us face to face
with one of the paradoxes of his thinking and with one of his abiding
concerns. As early as 1830, even before going to America, Tocqueville
worried in a letter to Charles Stoffels about a basic struggle in human society between individual strength (*la force individuelle*) and public power
(*la force publique*). How best to uphold the individual in the age of equality? The goal of encouraging the sufficiently forceful and independent
individual would never be far from his thinking. "In our times," he wrote
in a draft, "those who fear an excess of individualism are right, and those
who fear the extreme dependence of the individual are also right. Idea to
express somewhere *necessarily*."[16] As we have noted, Tocqueville's book
may be read as a study of how to preserve liberty during a time of advancing equality. But it may also be read as a reflection on how to promote
individual independence in democratic societies. Tocqueville wanted to
find the right balance between private strength and public power.

In another draft, he declared: "To sustain the individual in the face of
whatever social power, to conserve something for his independence, his
force, his originality; such must be the constant effort of all the friends of
humanity in democratic times. Just as in democratic times it is necessary
to elevate society and lower the individual."[17] The dilemma was inescapable: on the one hand, to foster individual independence; on the other, to
combat individualism.

In the 1835 text, Tocqueville carefully described how democracy de-
stroyed all traditional bonds and undermined the secondary bodies that

normally served as intermediaries between the lone individual and the forces of society writ large. The individual was first isolated, removed from all ties with class or even with successive generations of the same family, and then merged into the whole. So democracy tended constantly to weaken the individual and to strengthen the broad social power (and whatever or whoever claimed to represent that power). When "each citizen [is] equally powerless, equally poor, equally isolated," he asked, where would the demands of power stop? When the private person "can only oppose his individual weakness to the organized force of the government," what abuses might not be possible?[18]

While writing the 1840 *Democracy*, Tocqueville focused even more intently on the struggle between *la force individuelle* and *la force publique*. "Received and discovered beliefs, authority and liberty, individualism and social force are . . . needed at the same time. The whole question is to sort out the limits of these pairs. It is to that [question] that I must put all my mind."[19] In the margin, he noted the date: "24 April 1837." Here was the earliest use of the word *individualism* yet found in the working papers of Tocqueville's *Democracy*. And notice that in this draft passage Tocqueville actually introduced the term positively, linking it to liberty, and using it to express what he usually called *individual independence*. Elsewhere in the drafts and text of the 1840 portion of his book, he abandoned this initial usage and, as we have already noted, consistently presented individualism negatively. But once again, he had posed the essential democratic challenge: sorting out the limits between the individual and society as a whole.

The 1840 text summarized his thinking. "The political world is changing; henceforth one must seek new remedies for new ills. To fix extended, but visible and immovable, limits for social power; to give to particular persons certain rights and to guarantee them the uncontested enjoyment of these rights; to preserve for the individual the little independence, force, and originality that remain to him; to elevate him beside society and to sustain him before it: this appears to me to be the first object of the legislator in the age we are entering."[20] So Tocqueville's condemnation of democratic individualism did not mean a rejection of individual independence, which remained one of his essential goals.

But how did individualism threaten liberty? For Tocqueville *individualism* meant the habit of living isolated from your fellows, of not concerning yourself with any public affairs, and of abandoning those matters to the care of the government as the only clearly visible representative of common interests. Like democratic materialism, democratic individualism led to the death of civic life and opened the door to any despotic power that would assume responsibility for shared interests. Materialism deflected democratic people from public participation by attaching them to physical well-being; individualism, by luring them into their own small realm.

We need to recognize that, on the topic of individualism, Tocqueville once again treated the United States as something of an exception. He had described the American republic as shielded from the worst effects of democratic materialism; in his analysis, it was also insulated from individualism. First, Tocqueville pointed out that the Americans, who had supposedly not undergone a revolution, did not suffer from any lingering revolutionary spirit, which aggravated individualism, especially in France. Second, he argued that free institutions (especially associations, local liberties, and a free press) and the doctrine of interest well-understood accustomed the Americans to dealing with common interests and pushed them into the public arena.

The development of Tocqueville's idea of individualism also illustrates one of his most characteristic mental habits: the effort to sort out the limits of various conceptual pairs. Thinking in pairs and seeking out the point of equilibrium between opposing principles typify his way of thinking.

Finally, we should note that the structure of Tocqueville's 1840 chapters on materialism and individualism reveals another characteristic approach: his almost routine technique of first tracing the workings of an idea or principle in aristocratic societies, and then applying the same concept to democratic societies. This method allowed him, in a manner perhaps too abstract and deductive, to identify and explore the probable consequences of democracy. The second portion of his *Democracy* especially may be read, therefore, as a theoretical exploration of aristocracy and democracy as social types and as a running comparison of the two models.

CENTRALIZATION

See in vol. 1 (1835): part 1, chap. 4; part 2, chap. 1.

According to Tocqueville, democracy led to materialism, to individualism, and to centralization, or the concentration of power. Each of these,
in turn, put liberty at risk. The first two, by encouraging people to aban-
don public participation, left civic life to the control of others. But how
more directly did democracy favor centralization or the concentration
of power?

In his chapter on sovereignty of the people for the 1835 *Democracy*,
Tocqueville remarked: "In America, the principle of the sovereignty of
the people is not hidden or sterile as in certain nations; it is recognized
by mores, proclaimed by the laws; it spreads with freedom and reaches its
final consequences without obstacle." "The people," he concluded, "reign
over the American political world as does God over the universe. They
are the cause and the end of all things; everything comes out of them and
everything is absorbed into them."[21] Such God-like omnipotence deeply
troubled Tocqueville. In a draft he stated bluntly: "Despotism is attached
to omnipotence, whoever the representative may be."[22]

Contrary to the usual European opinion, democracy, Tocqueville
pointed out in his 1835 text, did not mean political weakness and anarchy.
He insisted on quite the opposite. "I do not think that the nature of democratic power is to lack force and resources; I believe, on the contrary,
that almost always the abuse of its strength . . . bring[s] it to perish."[23]
For him, the essential democratic danger was the accumulation of power,
which in turn threatened liberty.

But where exactly would power accumulate? Tocqueville devoted
much of his effort while writing to the task of identifying and describing for his readers the potentially despotic instruments of popular sovereignty. So *Democracy in America* may be read as a catalogue of what
Tocqueville understood as the many possible democratic despotisms. We
have already seen that in his treatment of materialism and individualism, he named one man alone, factions (or parties), and the government
as potential tyrants, all benefiting from democratic weaknesses. Tocqueville's list of possible culprits would grow.

WHERE WOULD POWER ACCUMULATE?

See in vol. 1 (1835): part 1, chap. 3, pp. 52–53; chap. 5, pp. 82–93; and chap. 8,
pp. 143–46; part 2, chaps. 1, 7, and 8; chap. 9, pp. 298–302; and chap. 10, pp. 379–84;
and in vol. 2 (1840): part 1, chap. 2; part 2, chap. 20; and part 4, chaps. 4 and 6.

Tocqueville argued that nations whose social state was democratic
tended to put power in the hands of whomever or whatever represented
(or claimed to represent) the people. In the 1835 *Democracy*, he identified
the first beneficiary of this inclination as the legislature. "Democracies,"
he noted, "are naturally brought to concentrate the whole social force in
the hands of the legislative body. The latter being the power that ema-
nates most directly from the people, it is also the one that participates
the most in its omnipotence. One therefore remarks a habitual tendency
in [the legislative body] that brings it to unite every kind of authority
within it."[24]

Tocqueville's warnings about legislative tyranny apparently arose first
from his concern about the ways in which many of the American state
constitutions made legislatures closely dependent on the people and then
put excessive power in the hands of legislators at the expense of the other
two branches of government. He also recalled the horrific excesses of
the National Convention during the French Revolution. And, when he
read *The Federalist Papers*, he found that James Madison echoed his own
misgivings about legislative power in democratic societies. "*Tyranny of
democracy.* Confusion of all powers in the hands of the *assemblies.* . . . See
very curious article of the *Federalist* on this subject . . . [number 48]."[25]

IN THE DRAFTS AND TEXT OF THE 1835 *DEMOCRACY* TOCQUE-
ville soon named a second, perhaps even more formidable beneficiary of the unlimited power of the people: the governmental administration.

> I am convinced, furthermore, that no nations are more at risk of falling un-
> der the yoke of administrative centralization than those whose social state is
> democratic. Several causes concur in this result. . . . The permanent ten-
> dency of these nations is to concentrate all governmental power in the

hands of the sole power that directly represents the people. . . . Now, when
the same power is already vested with all the attributes of government, it
is very difficult for it not to seek to enter into the details of administration,
and it hardly ever fails to find the occasion to do it in the long term. We
have been witnesses to this among ourselves.[26]

What did he mean by administrative centralization? Here we encounter one of his most important efforts to define his terms and to make
distinctions.

> Centralization is a word that is constantly repeated in our day and whose
> sense no one, in general, seeks to clarify. Nevertheless, two very distinct
> kinds of centralization exist, which it is important to know well. Certain
> interests are common to all parts of the nation, such as the formation of
> general laws and the relations of the people with foreigners. Other interests
> are special to certain parts of the nation, such as, for example, the under-
> takings of the township.
>
> To concentrate the power to direct the first in the same place or in the
> same hand is to found what I shall call governmental centralization. To
> concentrate the power to direct the second in the same manner is to found
> what I shall name administrative centralization.
>
> There are some points at which these two kinds of centralization come
> to be confused. But . . . one easily succeeds in distinguishing them.[27]

Despite his reassurances, the distinction between governmental and
administrative centralization was weak. Tocqueville himself recognized
that it did not work well; the two merged at many points, and more im-
portantly, he knew that concentrated governmental power ultimately
meant getting into administrative details. But distinguishing between the
two centralizations allowed Tocqueville, in the 1835 portion of his book,
to consider the democratic danger of administrative centralization.

What did he fear? What did he think might result from such administrative centralization? His descriptions in 1835 were chilling and strikingly foreshadowed his famous 1840 portrait of the "new democratic despotism." "It is understood," he wrote in the 1835 text, "that governmental
centralization acquires an immense force when it is joined to adminis-

trative centralization. In this manner, it habituates men . . . to obey, not once and on one point, but in everything and every day. It then not only subdues them by force, but it also captures them through their habits; it isolates them and afterwards fastens them one by one onto the common mass."[28]

Contrasting administrative centralization with the American system of decentralization, he asked: "What does it matter to me, after all, that there should be an authority always on its feet, keeping watch that my pleasures are tranquil, flying ahead of my steps to turn away every danger without my even needing to think about it, if this authority, at the same time that it removes the least thorns on my path, is absolute master of my freedom and my life, if it monopolizes movement and existence to such a point that everything around it must languish when it languishes, . . . sleep when it sleeps, . . . perish if it dies?"[29]

In both the 1835 and 1840 halves of his work, Tocqueville never wavered in his conviction that democracy and centralization went hand in hand. But if this assumption runs throughout his *Democracy*, his exploration of where power would accumulate and what kind of centralization most threatened democracies would lead to important changes between the two parts of his book. As we will see, Tocqueville's message about democratic despotisms would shift in significant ways between 1835 and 1840.

IN HIS 1835 TEXT TOCQUEVILLE OFFERED YET ANOTHER possible place, a third, where power would accumulate in democratic nations. We know that he sometimes worried about one man alone, clever and ambitious, seizing power and becoming a democratic despot. At times, he seemed to warn that the democratic choice between liberty and despotism was also a choice between government by all or "the yoke of one [man] alone."[30] "Now I know only two manners of making equality reign in the political world," he wrote in the 1835 portion of his book, "rights must be given to each citizen or to no one. For peoples who have reached the same social state as the Anglo-Americans, it is therefore very difficult to perceive a middle term between the sovereignty of all and the absolute power of one [man] alone."[31] For the moment, legislative tyranny and administrative centralization were set aside.

A draft explained more completely how democracy would usher in a tyrant. "How can we believe that the lower classes of society, nearly equal to the others in knowledge, more energetic than they, will put up with remaining excluded from the government? Can that possibly be imagined? Perhaps this will lead to the establishment of tyranny. Why democracy endures a tyrant rather than superiority of ranks and a hierarchy. Equality, dominant passion of democracies. Finish by this piece, men have only one way to be free, but they have two to be equal."[32]

In the pages of the 1835 *Democracy*, Tocqueville struggled to portray this new democratic despotism of the tyrant. As he drafted the subsection entitled "Importance of What Precedes in Relation to Europe,"[33] he reminded himself: "Here a portrait of the new tyranny, without counterbalance in the institutions, in the *mores*."[34] And in the text itself he declared: "If absolute power came to be established anew among the democratic peoples of Europe, I do not doubt that it would take a new form, and that it would show itself with features unknown to our fathers."[35]

But what would this new form be? Despotism in democracies would apparently resemble examples drawn from the "frightful centuries of Roman tyranny." In the end, Tocqueville, in his 1835 *Democracy*, could only reach back into ancient history to illustrate something of what he feared in the age of equality. Given all of the weaknesses of democratic societies, he admitted: "I feel myself brought to believe that there will soon no longer be room in [European nations] except for either democratic freedom or the tyranny of the Caesars."[36] Despite his assertions about a "new tyranny," Tocqueville in 1835 was as yet unable to depict anything truly novel. Not until 1840 would he succeed in portraying to his readers a genuinely new democratic despotism. And that portrait would show not the tyrant, but an unexpected version of administrative centralization.

Tocqueville's warnings to his countrymen were grim. But we need to recall here his insistence that a healthy democratic government could be established, that despotism was not inevitable. "I cannot believe," he confided to Louis de Kergorlay, "that for several centuries God has pushed two or three hundred million men toward equality of condition in order to bring them in the end to the despotism of Tiberius or Claudius."[37] Once again, Tocqueville's sense of the role of Providence in history colored his hopes for the future.

A FOURTH MAJOR DEMOCRATIC DESPOTISM APPEARED IN the pages of Tocqueville's 1835 *Democracy*: tyranny of the majority, one of the most famous and possibly the most controversial of his visions of despotism. In his discussion of the superiority of the federal constitution over those of the states, he described how, in the states, the unlimited power of the people was translated directly into legislative omnipotence. "This concentration of powers," he observed, ". . . founds the despotism of the majority."[38]

Apparently Jared Sparks of Boston, in September 1831, first suggested this idea to Tocqueville. During the following months Tocqueville repeatedly raised questions with other Americans about the power of the majority, the resulting dangers, and the possible remedies. He also kept a careful list of examples of abuses by the majority. And after returning to France, as he gathered his sources and prepared to write his book, he included among his organizing themes "Sovereignty of the people. Tyranny of the majority. Democracy, irresistible march of democracy."[39]

In the 1835 portion Tocqueville devoted two chapters to this particular democratic despotism.[40] In the first of the pair, "On the Omnipotence of the Majority in the United States and Its Effects," he made several essential points. He began as usual with the underlying principle: "It is of the very essence of democratic governments that the empire of the majority is absolute."[41] After analyzing how laws in the states and American customs, in general, enhanced the moral dominion of the majority, he declared: "The majority in the United States therefore has an immense power in fact, and a power in opinion almost as great."[42] This assertion included a definition of what tyranny of the majority meant for Tocqueville; it included both legal and political control ("an immense power in fact") and authority over opinion and thought ("a power in opinion almost as great"). This distinction is the first crucial point to note in his chapter.

Secondly, Tocqueville reminded his readers that tyranny of the majority, as he understood it, operated not on the federal or national level, but on the state level. It was in the states that constitutions and laws artificially enhanced rather than restrained the power of the majority.[43]

Thirdly and somewhat paradoxically, he wrote that only rarely did the democratic despotism of the majority operate in the United States. "I do not say that at the present time frequent use is made of tyranny in

America, I say that no guarantee against it may be discovered [there]."[44] So he conceded that tyranny of the majority was more potential than actual in America.

Despite this disclaimer, however, Tocqueville carefully presented, in the 1835 portion of his book, two painful instances of actual abuses by the majority, one relating to mob violence against antiwar editors during the War of 1812, and the other, to how free blacks in Pennsylvania were barred by physical threats from exercising their right to vote.[45] Significantly, these illustrations of tyranny of the majority as "power in fact" recounted incidents involving either times of war and national crisis or matters of race. A paragraph in Tocqueville's text directly reflected these examples. "When a man or a party suffers from an injustice in the United States, whom do you want him to address? Public opinion? that is what forms the majority; the legislative body? it represents the majority and obeys it blindly; the executive power? it is named by the majority and serves as its passive instrument; the public forces? the public forces are nothing other than the majority in arms; the jury? the jury is the majority vested with the right to pronounce decrees; in certain states, the judges themselves are elected by the majority. Therefore, however iniquitous or unreasonable is the measure that strikes you, you must submit to it."[46]

Yet the key argument in Tocqueville's treatment of tyranny of the majority probably relates not to "power in fact," but to "power in opinion." Certainly this was the part of his discussion that would emerge once again in 1840. In the United States, Tocqueville insisted, the majority exercised such power over thought and its expression that some ideas were never broached. "In America," he said flatly, "the majority draws a formidable circle around thought." His conclusions were equally blunt. "I do not know any country where, in general, less independence of mind and genuine freedom of discussion reign than in America." And "There is no freedom of mind in America."[47]

The omnipotence of the majority, according to Tocqueville, not only led to instances of violence and oppression, but also, more subtly and without physical force, it undermined intellectual independence and the free expression of ideas. This power over the mind, which worked better than the Inquisition, was what disturbed Tocqueville most.

Tocqueville firmly rejected the idea that the majority could do no wrong. For him, justice provided the essential check on the majority's power. "I regard as impious and detestable the maxim that in matters of government the majority of a people has the right to do everything, and nonetheless I place the origin of all powers in the will of the majority. Am I in contradiction with myself? A general law exists that has been made or at least adopted not only by the majority of this or that people, but by the majority of all men. This law is justice. Justice therefore forms the boundary of each people's right."[48]

In his 1835 *Democracy*, Tocqueville also lamented the "general abasement of souls" resulting from the majority's unlimited power and its need to be flattered and upheld.[49] His concerns about the loss of the "manly independence of thought"[50] and the corrosive moral effects of the omnipotence of the majority reappeared in the opening section of the 1840 portion of his work. In the chapter entitled "On the Principal Source of Beliefs Among Democratic Peoples," Tocqueville argued that in democratic societies intellectual authority rested with public opinion.

> As citizens become more equal and alike, the penchant of each to believe blindly a certain man or class diminishes. The disposition to believe the mass is augmented, and more and more it is opinion that leads the world.
>
> Not only is common opinion the sole guide that remains for individual reason among democratic peoples; but it has an infinitely greater power among these peoples than among any other. In times of equality, because of their similarity, men have no faith in one another; but this very similarity gives them an almost unlimited trust in the judgment of the public. . . . The public therefore has a singular power among democratic peoples, the very idea of which aristocratic nations could not conceive. It does not persuade . . . , it imposes [its beliefs] and makes them penetrate souls by a sort of immense pressure of the minds of all on the intellect of each.[51]

Tocqueville feared the loss of the ability and even the will to think; he worried that both intellectual liberty and creativity might be extinguished by the absolute power of the majority. "The majority," he wrote in a draft variant, "forces the human mind to stop, . . . and by forcing it constantly to obey, ends by taking away from it even the desire to be free to act for itself."[52]

In the 1840 text he concluded that the absolute power of the majority, "I cannot repeat too often, is something to cause profound reflection by those who see in the freedom of the intellect something holy, and who hate not only the despot but despotism. As for me, when I feel the hand of power weighing on my brow, it matters little to know who oppresses me, and I am no more disposed to put my head in the yoke because a million arms present it to me."[53]

The concept of tyranny of the majority illustrates for us how some of Tocqueville's most important ideas in the 1835 *Democracy* were carried forward and developed in new ways in the second portion of his book. In 1840, Tocqueville largely forgot the "power in fact" of the omnipotent majority. Instead, the "power in opinion," the pressure of public or mass opinion on intellectual freedom and on the very conception of new ideas, emerged as the focus of his fears.

We also find two fascinating paradoxes in Tocqueville's thinking about the absolute power of the majority. As we have seen, Tocqueville said in his 1835 chapter that tyranny of the majority in America was more a potential than an actual danger. At the same time, however, he declared categorically that no freedom of thought or discussion existed in the United States. These statements border on outright contradiction; but perhaps the distance between the two assertions measures the difference between the two sides of tyranny of the majority, power in fact and power in opinion, more than any opposition in Tocqueville's ideas about the reality of despotism of the majority. He seemed to be saying that legal or political abuses were rare, more potential than actual, but abuses of thought or opinion were observable and lethal. With that understanding the gap between his assertions fades.

Tocqueville argued forcefully as well, throughout both parts of his *Democracy* and especially in his 1835 discussion of the town and chapter on the federal constitution, that American decentralization and federalism were major supports for liberty in the United States. (We will return to this point later.) In his treatment of the omnipotence of the majority, however, he drew his illustrations of abuse from the cities and specifically reminded his readers that the danger of tyranny of the majority existed not on the national, but on the state, level. Again, we encounter a curious disjuncture. Tocqueville seemed to recognize that oppression, both violent and subtle, of the minority, of those who thought or looked differently, occurred more easily in the localities and states. Did his examples reveal a weakness in decentralization and federalism? Could the quasi-independent town be, instead of a refuge for liberty, a place where the worst prejudices of the majority could be expressed with impunity? Could a majority in a state more easily enact and enforce oppressive laws? He never asked himself or his readers to consider the possible implications of his argument about the majority's "power in fact."

Why has Tocqueville's concept of tyranny of the majority been so controversial? Some of the first American commentators on his book, including Jared Sparks, rejected it as mistaken. Others since have called it exaggerated or totally imaginary. And still other readers have charged Tocqueville with overlooking the real danger: tyranny of minorities—an unjust accusation, as we will see.

The idea of tyranny of the majority may be less persuasive if you focus on shifting political majorities, when no majority is safe from finding itself in the minority from one election to another. But if you focus on seemingly unchanging or very slowly changing majority opinions, attitudes, ideas, and prejudices, especially when the majority is more or less permanently exempt from how a minority is treated, the case is much stronger. As examples, among others, there is the whole matter of race in America, or the question of civil liberties and treatment of ethnic minorities in wartime or other times of national crisis. Considered from this perspective, Tocqueville's concept of the despotism of the majority becomes a key to understanding much of the long history of racial and ethnic injustice in America.[54]

TOCQUEVILLE'S GALLERY OF THREATS TO LIBERTY CHANGED somewhat in the 1840 *Democracy*. His earlier worry about legislative tyranny largely disappeared from the pages of his book. And his warnings about tyranny of the majority shifted by 1840 almost entirely to public or mass pressure on thought and opinion. But if some earlier dangers seemed to vanish and others were somewhat redefined, still others appeared for the first time. In the second portion of his *Democracy*

Tocqueville briefly introduced a new risk, tyranny of the minority. The democratic desire for order, he observed, could open the way to control not only by one man alone, but also by a faction or party. To that danger, he added the potential rise of an entirely new kind of oppressive minority, the manufacturing aristocracy.[55] (This is another topic we will revisit later.)

One image of despotism, the tyranny of one man alone, reemerged in 1840, but played a decidedly secondary role. Several times in the second part of his book, Tocqueville reminded his readers about the risk of the democratic despot. "A sort of equality," he observed in his chapter about how democratic peoples love equality more than liberty, "can even be established in the political world although there may be no political freedom. One might be equal to all those like him, except the one who is, without any distinction, the master of all."[56]

As Tocqueville wrote the 1840 *Democracy*, however, his concerns about the despot shifted from one man alone to a broader vision of military despotism. He probably modeled this variation on Napoleon and the centralizing tendencies of the Napoleonic state. One of the great dangers to liberty was war. In the 1840 text, Tocqueville elaborated:

> It is therefore principally in war that peoples feel the desire and often the need to increase the prerogatives of the central power. All geniuses of war love centralization, which increases their strength, and all centralizing geniuses love war, which obliges nations to draw tight all powers in the hands of the state. Thus, the democratic tendency that brings men constantly to multiply the privileges of the state and to restrict the rights of particular persons is much more rapid and more continuous in democratic peoples subject by their position to great and frequent wars, and whose existence can often be put in peril, than in all others.[57]

With these ideas in mind, Tocqueville offered a self-correction in his working papers. "When I said that there was no more aristocracy possible, I was mistaken; you can still have the aristocracy of men of war."[58] So the 1840 *Democracy* introduced, as dangerous minorities, not only factions and the manufacturing aristocracy, but also the "aristocracy of the men of war." Each one put liberty at risk.

ALTHOUGH TOCQUEVILLE CONTINUED TO CAUTION against the tyranny of one man alone, his primary warnings turned away from the idea of a democratic despot. Most significantly, he rejected his own 1835 warnings about the tyranny of the worst of the Caesars. That was not, he now realized, the most serious threat to liberty in democratic times. As Tocqueville wrote the 1840 *Democracy*, his thinking moved in a new direction.

Once again, he corrected himself and, in a draft dated March 7, 1838, sketched a different picture of democratic despotism.

> [If] men are enslaved, they will be so in an entirely new fashion and will exhibit a spectacle for which the past has not prepared us. . . . New society, regular, peaceful, ruled with art and uniformity, mixture of college, seminary, regiment, asleep rather than chained in the arms of clerks and soldiers, bureaucratic tyranny, fond of red tape, very repressive of all impulse, destroying the will for great things in germ, but mild and regular, equal for all. . . . That is the real and original picture. That of the first volume [the 1835 *Democracy*] was declamatory, common, hackneyed and false.[59]

In the 1840 text, as he began his chapter on "What Kind of Despotism Democratic Nations Have to Fear," he confirmed the transformation in his ideas.

> During my stay in the United States I had remarked that a democratic social state like that of the Americans could singularly facilitate the establishment of despotism, and I had seen on my return to Europe how most of our princes had already made use of the ideas, sentiments, and needs to which this same social state had given birth to extend the sphere of their power. That led me to believe that Christian nations would perhaps in the end come under an oppression similar to that which formerly weighed on several of the peoples of antiquity. A more detailed examination of the subject and five years of new meditations have not diminished my fears, but they have changed their object.[60]

Instead of the tyranny of Tiberius or Claudius, Tocqueville now envisioned something entirely different. In 1835 he had warned briefly about the effects of administrative centralization. By 1840 his critique evolved into a disturbing vision of a novel sort of soft or mild democratic despotism, the concentration of all power in the hands of the state or the bureaucracy.

Tocqueville realized that old words did not describe what he had in mind. Once again, as he did when considering individualism, Tocqueville searched for a new word to describe something entirely novel. But in this case, he did not succeed; if his portrait was strikingly original, he found no new label for what he envisioned. In the 1840 *Democracy* he admitted: "I think therefore that the kind of oppression with which democratic peoples are threatened will resemble nothing that has preceded it in the world; our contemporaries would not find its image in their memories. I myself seek in vain an expression that exactly reproduces the idea that I form of it for myself and that contains it; the old words of despotism and of tyranny are not suitable. The thing is new, therefore I must try to define it, since I cannot name it."[61]

But how to define the new democratic despotism? In July 1838, in a letter to his brother, Edouard, Tocqueville explained that he was busy writing what would become part 4 of the 1840 *Democracy* and sketched his working plan for the section.

> I begin by showing how, *theoretically*, [democratic] ideas and sentiments must facilitate the concentration of powers. Then I indicate what special and accidental circumstances can hasten or retard this tendency; which leads me to show that the greater part of these circumstances do not exist in America and exist in Europe. So I get to speaking about Europe and showing by *facts* how all European governments centralize constantly; how the power of the State always grows and that of individuals always diminishes. That leads me to define the type of democratic despotism which could arrive in Europe, and finally to examine in a general way what the tendencies of legislation must be to struggle against this tendency of the social condition.[62]

Tocqueville no longer insisted on his 1835 distinction between governmental and administrative centralization. He described the danger simply as the concentration of power in the hands of the sovereign power, the omnipotence of the state. This concentration of power subsumed both governmental and administrative centralization.

In various places in the 1840 portion of his book, Tocqueville presented additional characteristics of the new despotism. In one of his chapters on the taste for well-being, for example, he asserted: "The nature of absolute power in democratic centuries is neither cruel nor savage, but it is minute and vexatious."[63] But finally, in the 1840 text, in one of the most famous and most chilling passages of his book, Tocqueville presented a full portrait of the new democratic despotism. The importance of this segment for understanding Tocqueville's message must be my excuse for presenting such a long quotation from his *Democracy*:

> I want to imagine with what new features despotism could be produced in the world; I see an innumerable crowd of like and equal men who revolve on themselves without repose, procuring the small and vulgar pleasures with which they fill their souls.
>
> . . . Above these an immense tutelary power is elevated, which alone takes charge of assuring their enjoyments and of watching over their fate. It is absolute, detailed, regular, far-seeing and mild. It would resemble paternal power if, like that, it had for its object to prepare men for manhood; but on the contrary, it seeks only to keep them fixed irrevocably in childhood; it likes the citizens to enjoy themselves, provided that they think only of enjoying themselves. It willingly works for their happiness; but it wants to be the unique agent and sole arbiter of that; it provides for their security, foresees and secures their needs, facilitates their pleasures, conducts their principal affairs, directs their industry, regulates their estates, divides their inheritances; can it not take away from them entirely the trouble of thinking and the pain of living? . . .
>
> [After] taking each individual by turns in its powerful hands and kneading him as it likes, the sovereign extends its arms over society as a whole; it covers its surface with a network of small, complicated, painstaking, uniform rules, through which the most original minds and the most vigorous souls cannot clear a way to surpass the crowd; it does not break wills, but it softens them, bends them and directs them; it rarely forces one to act, but it constantly opposes itself to one's acting; it does not destroy, it prevents things from being born; it does not tyrannize, it hinders, compromises, enervates, extinguishes, dazes, and finally reduces each nation to being nothing more than a herd of timid and industrious animals of which the government is the shepherd.[64]

This striking image, which echoes much of what Tocqueville wrote about individualism and materialism as putting liberty at risk, serves as a kind of summary of the potential dangers of democracy. In particular, the moral implications of the new democratic despotism need to be acknowledged. Once again, Tocqueville the moralist comes to the fore. Although mild or soft, the new despotism was thorough, intrusive, and ensnaring. The minute and pervasive bureaucratic supervision and regulation ultimately turned citizens into children. By smoothing the way, by removing all difficulties, the state ended by undermining individual independence and any possible social, political, or intellectual vitality. (Tocqueville's short discussion in 1835 of the consequences of administrative centralization made much the same argument.) In the moral terms that Tocqueville often used, the springs of action were relaxed; souls, weakened; and human grandeur, undermined. What he always seemed to fear most were the moral consequences of the loss of liberty.

Here a word of caution. Although Tocqueville denounced administrative despotism and warned readers about the tutelary or shepherd state, we need to recognize that he did not oppose active government or centralized power as such. He knew that centralization had its advantages. "Contained within certain limits," he wrote in a draft, "centralization is a necessary fact, and I add that it is a fact about which we must be glad. A strong and intelligent central power is one of the first necessities in centuries of equality. Acknowledge it boldly."[65] The prosperity of a nation, he argued, requires the execution of great national enterprises; such large and costly works were essential to the public good and, in turn, required a centralized state. So Tocqueville's views about centralization and the appropriate role of government were nuanced and complex; we will examine them more fully below.

TOCQUEVILLE'S PORTRAIT OF THE NEW DEMOCRATIC DESpotism has been read in different ways. In the mid-twentieth century his portrayal was widely understood as a brilliant, even prophetic depiction of the stultifying tyranny of the totalitarian regimes of twentieth-century fascism and communism. During the last forty years, it has often been interpreted as a warning, especially to the United States and the nations of Western Europe, about the expanding welfare state, with its intrusive bureaucracy and constant intervention in the daily lives of citizens. Some readers even assume that Tocqueville's vision depicts an inevitable consequence of advancing democracy and illustrates the ultimate demise of liberty in the face of an always unsatisfied and insistent equality. Still others read the passages and weep, believing we are already ensnared in the trap described by Tocqueville.

A careful examination of his working papers for the final part of his 1840 book demonstrates, however, that the image of the new democratic despotism is primarily a dystopia, an imagined worst-case scenario for France, should the easy tendency toward state intervention in all economic and industrial undertakings remain unchecked. Tocqueville's portrait is a caution about a terrible world that might emerge from democracy, not a statement about either a current reality or a necessary result of equality. Our review of Tocqueville's convictions has already noted his rejection of determined outcomes.

Although Tocqueville's portrait of the new democratic despotism is now commonly cited in discussions about political life in the United States, we should remember that when he wrote his 1840 description he did not have America in mind. His drafts and other working papers demonstrate how thoroughly political and economic debates in France during the late 1830s, especially those about the proper role of the state in major economic enterprises, shaped his view of what type of despotism was to be feared. Tocqueville even remarked that the American situation was singular; Americans had never needed the government to intervene in detail in their affairs. "On this point," he declared, "the Americans, whatever their errors and their faults, deserve to be praised. They have well earned humanity's gratitude. They have shown that the democratic social state and democratic laws did not have as a necessary result the degeneration of the human race. I am very content to have found this idea because I believe it correct and because it is the only way to make *America* appear a final time in my last chapters, which really relate only to France."[66]

A S WE HAVE SEEN, TOCQUEVILLE'S PRESENTATION OF democratic despotisms changed significantly from 1835 to 1840. In the first part of his *Democracy* Tocqueville tended to describe liberty in democratic societies as threatened either by the despotism of the many or by that of one man alone. Although in his conclusion he offered a dramatic warning about the tyranny of the worst of the Caesars, the most original and important image of democratic despotism found in the 1835 portion was tyranny of the majority, a particularly American despotism, according to Tocqueville. The idea of the return of Tiberius or Claudius was largely meant to reawaken France, but by 1840 Tocqueville realized that this threat was empty.

In 1840 Tocqueville revisited the power of the many over thought and opinion, continued to warn against the tyrant, and even introduced a more original vision of military despotism. But the new democratic despotism of the state, which Tocqueville presented as a particularly French danger, clearly became the most significant image of democratic tyranny in the second part of his work. This shift in emphasis among the varieties of despotism paralleled the broader shift between 1835 and 1840 from a book focused primarily on America to one focused primarily on democracy.

In his discussions of materialism, individualism, and the new democratic despotism, Tocqueville treated America as an exception in much of the 1840 *Democracy*. He also increasingly resorted to three-way comparisons, measuring France, England, and America against each other. This tendency to cast the American situation as singular and to present England, more frequently, as another useful point of reference reflects as well how much the second portion of his work moved away from America.

As his book became less American, his images of the major democratic despotism facing France (and Europe) became notably more original and darker. Gone were Tiberius and Claudius. In place of Caesar came the tutelary state, the government as shepherd. But at least in the pages of his *Democracy*, he never succumbed entirely to pessimism. Remember that he concluded his book by reassuring his readers and describing a large circle within which they could still make choices, take action, and accept responsibility for preserving their own liberty.

Did the many despotisms envisioned by Tocqueville share some common trait? In his book he warned passionately not only against the specific threat of administrative centralization, but also against the broader danger of consolidated power, no matter where that power was concentrated, whether in public or private institutions, whether in the hands of the people, the majority, the mass, public opinion, the legislature, the military leader, one man alone, the bureaucracy, the state, or even the manufacturing aristocracy or some faction. All of these possible centers of consolidated power worried Tocqueville.

What most fundamentally threatened liberty? Unchecked and unlimited power was at the core of his warnings. In the 1835 text he observed:

> I think, therefore, that one must always place somewhere one social power superior to all the others, but I believe freedom to be in peril when that power finds no obstacle before it that can restrain its advance and give it time to moderate itself. Omnipotence seems to me to be an evil and dangerous thing in itself. Its exercise appears to me above the strength of man, whoever he may be, and I see only God who can be omnipotent without danger, because his wisdom and justice are always equal to his power. There is therefore no authority on earth so respectable in itself or vested with a right so sacred that I should wish to allow to act without control or to dominate without obstacles. Therefore, when I see the right and the ability to do everything granted to any power whatsoever, whether it is called people or king, democracy or aristocracy, whether it is exercised in a monarchy or a republic, I say: there is the seed of tyranny, and I seek to go live under other laws.[67]

Democracy invited omnipotence. And Tocqueville believed that any authority or agent of power, if not restrained or limited in some way, posed a potential danger to liberty. Here was one of his bedrock political principles.

6

How to Preserve Liberty?

See in vol. 2 (1840): part 4, chap. 7.

W E ALREADY KNOW THAT FOR TOCQUEVILLE LIBERTY evoked both laws—certain legal, institutional, and constitutional arrangements—and mores—certain ingrained behaviors, habits, ideas, attitudes, values, and beliefs. His recommendations for preserving freedom consistently reflected the same two dimensions: laws and mores. Throughout his book, what may be described as Tocqueville's political program, broadly understood, included proposals for fostering both *free institutions* and *habits of liberty* (or *habits of freedom*). We will also see once again that one of his enduring principles was to cure democracy by using more democracy.

Tocqueville remained clear about his own purposes. As he began the second part of the 1840 *Democracy*, entitled "Influence of Democracy on the Sentiments of the Americans," he reminded himself in a draft:

> Ideas that must never be entirely lost from view. After making known each flaw or each quality inherent in democracy, try to point out with as much *precision* as possible the means that can be taken to attenuate the first and to develop the second. *Example.* Men in democracies are naturally led to concentrate on their interests. To draw them away from their interests as much as possible, to spiritualize them as much as possible, and finally if possible to connect and merge particular interest and general interest, so that you scarcely know how to distinguish the one from the other. That is the political side of the work that must never be allowed to be entirely lost from view.

And always mindful of the reactions of his readers, he added: "But do not do that in a monotonous and tiring way, for fear of boredom, or in too practical and too detailed a way, for fear of leaving myself open to criticism."[1]

Notably, in his example of the political side of his work, Tocqueville referred, at least by implication, to local liberties and associations (to draw people away from their own narrow interests), to religion (to spiritualize), and to interest well understood (to connect and merge particular and general interest). These key elements of his political program, which we will examine more fully in a moment, were constantly foremost in his thinking.

In the 1840 text, in two brief sentences, he presented another remarkable summary of the political side of his work. "There is no question of reconstructing an aristocratic society, but of making freedom issue from the bosom of the democratic society in which God makes us live. These two first truths seem to me simple, clear and fertile, and they naturally lead me to consider what kind of free government can be established in a people where conditions are equal."[2]

What type of free government did he suggest? How best to make liberty emerge from democratic society? Here were the essential political questions for Tocqueville. His proposals, many of which we have already encountered, need to be enumerated in as succinct a way as possible. Moving almost chapter by chapter through the 1835 *Democracy*, we see what he presented in the category of laws broadly understood: local liberties, decentralization, and the principle of scattering power (exemplified by the New England town); broad suffrage and self-government; checks and balances among the three branches of government, an active and independent judiciary, bicameralism, and special use of indirect election (as modeled in the American federal constitution); liberty of the press; associations, the right of association, and freedom to speak, write, and assemble; individual rights; the jury system; and separation of church and state.

These *free institutions*, as Tocqueville often called them, were also mentioned throughout his travel notebooks and letters written from America. What he presented as safeguards for liberty in the 1835 *Democracy* drew heavily from his American experience; what he did not discover in the New World was at least witnessed and evaluated there as a live or actual example of what could be done to preserve freedom.

And in the broad category of mores, he offered the spirit of religion, the spirit of locality, the spirit of association, practical political experience, general enlightenment, a sense of justice, respect for law, respect for the rights of others, private morality, public spirit, a sense of the larger public good, and an understanding of how private and public interest merged. These attitudes, beliefs, and behaviors constituted what Tocqueville meant by the *habits of liberty*, and once again they were apparent from the moment of his arrival in the New World, in his travel diaries, in his letters home, and in the successive drafts and final text of the 1835 *Democracy*.

The 1840 *Democracy* largely repeated these recommendations for both the laws and mores that could safeguard freedom. In his penultimate chapter, Tocqueville offered perhaps the best single summary in detail of what he proposed for assuring a free democratic society. The chapter, entitled simply "Continuation of the Preceding Chapters," is largely a list of most of the important elements in his political program, including decentralization, associations, freedom of the press, an independent judiciary, and individual rights.[3]

Looking closely at each of the many proposals in the political side of Tocqueville's *Democracy* is impossible in any short format. Instead we will focus on four of the most significant and recurring elements in his political program: decentralization, associations, the doctrine of interest well understood (or self-interest well understood), and religion. These four will serve to illustrate the characteristic ways in which Tocqueville's ideas developed and his book took shape.

DECENTRALIZATION

See in vol. 1 (1835): part 1, chap. 5, especially pp. 82–93; part 2, chap. 6, pp. 231–35.

Tocqueville arrived in the New World already attuned to the issue of centralization, which was a matter of great political interest in France during the 1820s. But he was astonished to see to what extent the Americans, relying on shared efforts within the local community, did without government. As early as June 1831, he wrote to his father: "With us the government is involved in everything. [Here] there is no, or at least there doesn't appear to be any government at all. All that is good in centralization seems to be as unknown as what is bad. No central idea whatsoever seems to regulate the movement of the machine."[4] The United States presented an extreme case of administrative decentralization; yet the nation functioned and flourished. Tocqueville was fascinated.

During September and October 1831, in Boston, Tocqueville heard repeatedly about the importance of the towns as bedrock institutions for local self-government in the American republic. Jared Sparks spoke particularly about the *spirit of locality* as a characteristic attitude, at least among New Englanders. Perhaps more significantly, from his conversations in Boston, Tocqueville learned that if a lack of central government led to certain administrative inefficiencies, local liberties had undeniable social and political advantages. Local liberties promoted a sense of the common good and habits of shared initiative and participation in public life.

Once again Tocqueville carried these lessons directly into the 1835 *Democracy*. After discussing the spirit of the town (or township) in New England, he remarked: "What most strikes the European who travels through the United States is the absence of what is called among us government or administration. In America you see written laws; you perceive their daily execution; everything moves around you, and nowhere do you discover the motor. The hand that directs the social machine vanishes at each instant."[5] Much of the responsibility for moving the social machine in America, he realized, rested with the localities.

In one of the most important subsections of the 1835 *Democracy*, "On the Political Effects of Administrative Decentralization in the United States," Tocqueville presented not only praise for local liberties, but also his argument for less administrative centralization in France. He conceded the administrative flaws in decentralization, but stressed how local liberties enhanced the spirit of citizenship, promoted participation in shared enterprises, spread practical political experience, and ultimately produced greater social and political vitality.[6] The American voyage had provided Tocqueville with firsthand evidence to argue that decentralization need not be so feared in France. In the ongoing debate at home, he became an eyewitness to what was possible and an advocate for the gradual reinvigoration of local and provincial institutions.

ASSOCIATIONS

See in vol. 1 (1835): part 2, chaps. 2, 3, and 4; and in vol. 2 (1840):
part 2, chaps. 5, 6, and 7; and part 4, chap. 7.

During his journey Tocqueville was also amazed by the associational activity in the United States. He filled his travel diaries with conversations, examples, and reflections about associations and the American habit of association. In one of his notebooks, he remarked: "The spirit of association . . . is one of the distinctive characteristics of America; it is by this means that a country, where capital is scarce and where absolutely democratic laws and habits hinder the accumulation of wealth in the hands of a few individuals, has already succeeded in carrying out undertakings and accomplishing works which the most absolute kings and the most opulent aristocracies would certainly not have been able to undertake and finish in the same time."[7] Associations allowed the Americans to bring forth wonders, and as Tocqueville had already noticed, to some degree they took the place of "opulent aristocracies."

In the 1835 portion of his *Democracy*, in the chapter on associations, Tocqueville introduced several themes about associations that would remain fundamental throughout his book. It is essential at the outset to notice Tocqueville's broad definition of association. He included "permanent associations created by law under the names of townships, cities, and counties," as well as "a multitude of others that owe their birth and development only to individual will."[8] The former are often overlooked. Readers of Tocqueville's *Democracy* usually think of associations as primarily all kinds of private, ad hoc, and more or less temporary groups. Tocqueville, however, folded both types into associational life.

After defining his terms, Tocqueville next described the astonishing number and variety of associations in the United States. "America is, among the countries of the world, the one where they have taken most advantage of association and where they have applied that powerful mode of action to a greater diversity of objects. . . . In the United States, they associate for the goals of public security, of commerce and industry, of morality and religion. There is nothing the human will despairs of attaining by the free action of the collective power of individuals."[9]

Americans formed associations out of habit; they displayed an almost instinctive spirit of association. In his 1835 text, taking an illustration directly from a conversation with Josiah Quincy recorded in his travel notebooks, Tocqueville described the American impulse to associate. "An obstacle comes up on the public highway, passage is interrupted, traffic stops; the neighbors immediately establish themselves in a deliberating body; from this improvised assembly will issue an executive power that will remedy the ill—before the idea of an authority preexisting that of those interested has presented itself to anyone's imagination."[10]

In the 1835 chapter he focused on political associations—parties and political gatherings—and argued that liberty of the press and the freedoms to write and to assemble were connected to the right of association. Newspapers expressed and spread ideas, developed a community of opinion, and supported political associations, which in turn put people with similar ideas and opinions in touch with each other, overcame their sense of isolation, and allowed a challenge to the moral power of the majority. For Tocqueville, as we noted, associations functioned as democratic substitutes for the powerful individuals who had existed in aristocratic societies.

After reminding his readers about the connection between town liberties and associations, he declared in the 1835 text:

> There are no countries where associations are more necessary to prevent the despotism of parties or the arbitrariness of the prince than those in which the social state is democratic. In aristocratic nations, secondary bodies form natural associations that halt abuses of power. In countries where such associations do not exist, if particular persons cannot create artificially and temporarily something that resembles [those natural associations], I no longer perceive a dike of any sort against tyranny, and a great people can be oppressed with impunity by a handful of factious persons or by one man.[11]

In his chapter Tocqueville also expressed his reservations about an un-limited right of political association in France and other societies where suffrage was extremely narrow. In such nations, unchecked liberty of as-sociation could spawn secret revolutionary political groups claiming to speak for a majority shut out of political participation. The United States, he pointed out, avoided this problem by having very broad suffrage. No small political group could legitimately claim to represent a silent ma-jority. So Tocqueville's support for the right of association blended with an argument for wider suffrage. In a few short pages he linked liberty of association, freedom of the press, and the right to vote. Such close intertwining of his proposals marked his political program for a free government.

In 1840 Tocqueville shifted his attention to civil associations, but largely repeated the themes of 1835. He once again admitted that he found the variety of associations in the United States amazing. In the 1840 por-tion of his book, however, Tocqueville presented a more complete theory of association. "Thus the [United States] is found to be, above all, the [country] where men in our day have most perfected the art of pursuing the object of their common desires in common and have applied this new science to the most objects. . . . In democratic countries the science of as-sociation is the mother science; the progress of all the others depends on the progress of that one."[12]

In his penultimate chapter he declared:

> I firmly believe that one cannot found an aristocracy anew in the world; but I think that when plain citizens associate, they can constitute very opulent, very influential, very strong beings—in a word, aristocratic persons. In this manner one would obtain several of the greatest political advantages of aristocracy, without its injustices or dangers. A political, industrial, com-mercial, or even scientific and literary association is an enlightened and powerful citizen whom one can neither bend at will nor oppress in the dark and who, in defending its particular rights against the exigencies of power, saves common freedoms.[13]

Associations not only functioned as artificial substitutes in democra-cies for the groupings natural to aristocracies, but they also overcame the isolation and weakness of individuals in democratic societies. "Sentiments and ideas renew themselves, the heart is enlarged, and the human mind is developed only by the reciprocal action of men upon one another. I have shown that this action is almost nonexistent in a democratic country. It is therefore necessary to create it artificially there. And this is what associations alone can do."[14]

So the theme of the science or art of association is one of the most constant of Tocqueville's ideas. His focus did change from political associations in 1835 to civil associations in 1840, but this shift, which was part of the planned structure of his book, was done very consciously, with clear notification to his readers. Nonetheless, his treatment of associations—his explanation of why they were so important in democratic societies—was essentially unchanging. And once again much of the inspiration and evidence for his theory of association was what he had seen in America.

We have also noticed Tocqueville's expansive definition of association; he included not only political parties and commercial or other corporations, but also permanent and legally constituted entities such as towns, cities, and counties, as well as the voluntary associations so cherished by Americans. Understood in this manner, local liberties become simply one type of associational activity and one instrument for creating artificially what Tocqueville called "aristocratic persons." So if Tocqueville praised decentralization as a mechanism for scattering power in society, he also recommended it as a way to multiply associations.

SELF-INTEREST WELL UNDERSTOOD

See in vol. 1 (1835): part 2, chap. 6, pp. 225–27; and in vol. 2 (1840):
part 2, chaps. 8, 9, and 14.

Tocqueville's concept of *self-interest well understood,* or simply *interest well understood* (*intérêt bien entendu*) stands as an excellent example of how his ideas developed gradually over a period of years, from initial musings stimulated by what he saw in America in 1831, to first mention in drafts and text of the 1835 *Democracy,* and then to full presentation of a complete social and philosophical theory in the 1840 portion of his work. The story of how this idea of interest well understood emerged also reveals an extended dialogue between Tocqueville and Montesquieu, one of the major sources of his approach and thought.

Within weeks of arriving in the New World, Tocqueville grasped the special role played by *interest* in the American republic. Interest seemed to be the glue that held together an incredibly diverse population. And not only were particular interest and the general interest "never contrary," but also *interest* dared to proclaim itself a social theory.[15] Tocqueville soon discovered what, in the 1835 *Democracy*, he would call one of the bedrock principles of American society: "[the] maxim that the individual is the best as well as the only judge of his particular interest."[16]

At the same time, however, Americans seemed to have a profound understanding of the broader common interest.

> Another point which America demonstrates is that virtue is not, as has long been claimed, the only thing that maintains republics [argued by Montesquieu among others], but that enlightenment, more than any other thing, makes this social condition easy. The Americans are scarcely more virtuous than others; but they are infinitely more enlightened (I speak of the masses) than any other people I know; . . . the body of people who have understanding of public affairs, knowledge of the laws and of precedents, feeling for the well understood interests [*intérêts bien entendus*] of the nation, and the faculty to understand them, is greater than in any other place in the world.[17]

Perhaps the way in which the Americans managed to blend private and public interest most surprised Tocqueville. He quickly became aware that what he was seeing in the New World challenged some of the traditional categories familiar to him. During the first month of his journey, he wrote in his travel diaries:

> Ancient republics operated on the principle that the particular interest was to be sacrificed to the general good, and in this sense one can say that these republics were *virtuous*. The principle of this republic seems to me to be to require the particular interest to serve the general interest. A sort of refined and intelligent egotism appears to be the axis about which the whole

machine revolves. These people do not trouble to find out whether public virtue is good, but they claim to prove that it is useful. If the latter point is true, as I believe to some degree it is, this society can pass for enlightened, but not virtuous. But to what degree are the two principles of individual good and general good compatible? . . . Only the future can tell us.[18]

Tocqueville realized that the American example required a revision or recasting of Montesquieu. In a draft of the 1835 *Democracy* he observed:

> Of virtue in republics. The Americans are not a virtuous people and yet they are free. This does not absolutely prove that virtue . . . is not essential to the existence of republics. The idea of Montesquieu must not be taken in a narrow sense. . . . What he means by virtue is the moral power that each individual exercises over himself and that prevents him from violating the right of others. When this triumph of man over temptation is the result of the weakness of the temptation or of a calculation of personal interest, it does not constitute virtue in the eyes of the moralist; but it is included in the idea of Montesquieu who spoke of the effect much more than of the cause. In America it is not virtue that is great, it is temptation that is small, which comes to the same thing. It is not disinterestedness that is great, it is interest that is well understood, which again comes back to almost the same thing. So Montesquieu was right although he spoke about ancient virtue, and what he says of the Greeks and Romans is still applicable to the Americans.[19]

Although the term appeared in his travel notes and drafts, Tocqueville would seldom use the phrase *self-interest well understood* (or *interest well understood*) in the 1835 *Democracy*. Instead he pointed out how general enlightenment checked excessive egoism and stressed the harmony between private and public interest that prevailed in the United States.[20] But it is important to recognize that the concept of interest well understood had emerged long before Tocqueville began to write the 1840 portion of his book.

In the 1840 text this "intelligent egotism" and this blending of private and public interest—this new kind of virtue—would be explicitly labeled the doctrine of self-interest well understood. In the chapter devoted to the idea, Tocqueville wrote: "I have already shown in several places in this work how the inhabitants of the United States almost always know how to combine their own well-being with that of their fellow citizens. What I want to remark here is the general theory by the aid of which they come to this."[21] "[The] Americans," he remarked elsewhere in his text, "have so to speak reduced selfishness [egoism] to a social and philosophical theory."[22]

To govern men in democratic times, Tocqueville argued, new virtues were needed. Among the virtues he had in mind was the doctrine of self-interest well understood. In the 1840 text he asserted: "I shall not fear to say that the doctrine of self-interest well understood seems to me of all philosophical theories the most appropriate to the needs of men in our time, and that I see in it the most powerful guarantee against themselves that remains to them. The minds of the moralists of our day ought to turn, therefore, principally toward it. Even should they judge it imperfect, they would still have to adopt it as necessary."[23]

Clearly Tocqueville knew that the doctrine of interest well understood was more of a substitute for virtue than a true virtue, but it served nonetheless as a useful revision of traditional assumptions in general and of Montesquieu in particular. For Tocqueville, self-interest well understood stood as an American inspired check on democratic individualism and, as such, a major protection for liberty in democratic societies. It brought people out of their narrow private spheres and encouraged engagement with common interests and participation in public life; and it helped to turn individuals into citizens.

Tocqueville's concept is usually understood simply as enlightened self-interest or self-interest properly understood. But we should recall that, for Tocqueville, interest well understood included understanding *both* private and public interest well. The habitual blending of the two is what especially fascinated him about American behavior. Although the concept involved a "refined and intelligent egotism," it moved beyond enlightened self-interest because it also assumed a kind of informed and preexisting grasp of what the larger public interest was in the first place. It rested on a broad understanding of both private and public interest and recognition of the need for harmony and collaboration between the two.

RELIGION

See in vol. 1 (1835): Tocqueville's introduction, esp. pp. 10–12; part 1, chap. 2;
part 2, chap. 9, pp. 275–88; and in vol. 2 (1840): part 1, chaps. 1, 5, 6, and 7;
part 2, chaps. 9, 12, 15, and 17; part 4, chap. 8.

For Tocqueville religion served as another essential protection for liberty
in democratic societies. Religion, he argued in his *Democracy*, "spiritual-
ized" human beings who were tempted to concentrate all their time and
energy on material gain and physical comfort. And it set moral bound-
aries on potential democratic social and political excesses.[24] Tocqueville
insisted throughout his book that democratic societies needed to be
grounded in religious faith if liberty was to survive. But were democracy
and religion compatible?

After reviewing the early colonial history of New England, Tocqueville, as we have already seen, described one of the defining characteristics of Anglo-American civilization as the marvelous blending of the
spirit of religion and the *spirit of freedom*.[25] This novel combination—a
lesson drawn from the Puritan origins of the American republic—was
entirely unexpected. In France the forces of liberty and those of religion
seemed at war; so the example of a thoroughly democratic society where
religion exercised such moral influence amazed Tocqueville. "The philosophers of the eighteenth century," he noted, "explained the gradual
weakening of beliefs in an altogether simple fashion. Religious zeal, they
said, will be extinguished as freedom and enlightenment increase." With
sarcasm, he added: "It is unfortunate that the facts do not accord with this
theory. . . . On my arrival in the United States, it was the religious aspect
of the country that first struck my eye."[26]

But how was the spirit of religion sustained in America? Here Tocqueville made another unexpected discovery. He found that one of the primary causes of the outward power that religion continued to have in
the United States was the careful separation of church and state.[27] Religious beliefs and attitudes were part of what he meant by mores, but for
Tocqueville maintaining the strength of religion also involved particular
laws or institutional arrangements. The main cause for the weakness of
Christianity in Europe, he wrote in the 1835 *Democracy*, was "the intimate

union of politics and religion. . . . In Europe, Christianity has permitted itself to be intimately united with the powers of the earth. Today those powers are falling and [Christianity] is almost buried under their debris. It is a living [thing] that someone wanted to attach to the dead; cut the bonds that hold it back and it will rise again."[28]

In the 1840 *Democracy* Tocqueville argued even more emphatically in favor of separation of church and state. "[As] for state religions, I have always thought that if sometimes they could temporarily serve the interests of political power, they would always sooner or later become fatal to the Church. . . . I feel myself so sensitive to the almost inevitable dangers that beliefs risk when their interpreters mix in public affairs, and I am so convinced that one must maintain Christianity within the new democracies at all cost, that I would rather chain priests in the sanctuary than allow them to leave it."[29]

Tocqueville's consistent advocacy of separation of church and state and his concurrent desire to blend the spirit of religion and the spirit of liberty set him and his political program apart. As he explained in his 1835 introduction, he wanted to bring together open-minded men of good will, including both those believers who cherished liberty and those champions of freedom who recognized the value of religious faith. This effort to end the division between democracy and faith that prevailed in France and to build a new political alliance counted as still another purpose of Tocqueville's *Democracy*.

As we know, Tocqueville's personal religious faith, his belief in Roman Catholic doctrine, largely dissolved when he first read some of the leading figures of the French Enlightenment. Yet he continued to defend Christianity as the most sublime and self-evident religion, as the one most compatible with advancing equality, and even as the source for the belief in the fundamental equality of human beings.[30]

But according to Tocqueville, enlarging human souls and elevating human striving beyond the material world were among the most fundamental needs in democratic times. For achieving these goals, he believed that religious faith of almost any kind was better than none. "[I am convinced]," he wrote years later in a letter to his friend Francisque de Corcelle, "that man's true grandeur lies only in the harmony of liberal

sentiment and religious sentiment, both working simultaneously to ani-
mate and to restrain souls; . . . [my] sole political passion for thirty years
has been to bring about this harmony."[31] This letter, curiously echoing
what he said in the second chapter of the 1835 *Democracy*, underscores
the persistence of Tocqueville's convictions about the role of religion and
the consistency of the argument that he presented so forcefully from the
opening pages of his book.[32]

W̲HAT DOES OUR EXAMINATION OF TOCQUEVILLE'S PRE-
scriptions for free democratic government tell us? As we have
seen, the political program presented in his book was largely suggested
or reinforced by what he had learned in America. But he did not recom-
mend duplicating New World laws and institutions. American lessons, he
insisted, had to be interpreted broadly and adapted appropriately. "Those
who, after having read this book, judged that in writing it I wanted to
propose Anglo-American laws and mores for imitation by all peoples
who have a democratic social state would have committed a great error; they would have become attached to the form, abandoning the very
substance of my thought. My goal has been to show, by the example of
America, that laws and above all mores can permit a democratic people
to remain free. I am, for the rest, very far from believing that we ought
to follow the example that American democracy has given and to imitate
the means it has used to attain that goal by its efforts; . . . I would regard it
as a great misfortune for the human race if freedom had to be produced
with the same features in all places."[33]

Tocqueville did not expect his French readers in particular to tolerate any hint of remaking their government to imitate the United States.
Such an idea would offend national sensibilities, and his readers would
accuse him of succumbing to the American example, of being seduced
by what he had seen in the New World. Nor, when his work was published, would they be willing to accept a republic. Tocqueville himself
also rejected federalism as inappropriate for the exposed geopolitical position of France. And most fundamentally, he believed that any political
structures had to reflect the society in which they were found. Again, as
we have noted, laws, for Tocqueville, had to harmonize with mores. No

particular governmental institutions were absolutely good or universally transportable.

Perhaps most striking is the persistence, during the entire course of the writing of his book, of the major elements of his political program. The concept of self-interest well understood arguably emerged more strongly in the second portion of *Democracy in America* than in the first portion. But overall Tocqueville's list of remedies for curing democratic ills remained relatively unchanged between 1835 and 1840. Indeed the consistency of the "political side" of Tocqueville's message serves as one of the best proofs of the unity of the two parts of his work.

WHAT IS TOCQUEVILLE'S ESSENTIAL MESSAGE?

See in vol. 1 (1835): part 2, chap. 6, pp. 231–35, and chap. 9, pp. 298–302;
and in vol. 2 (1840): part 4, chaps. 7 and 8.

Are Tocqueville's political proposals, as they appear in *Democracy in America*, tied together by any common threads? On October 5, 1836, Tocqueville, in a letter, replied to his friend, Eugène Stoffels, who had expressed suspicion of Tocqueville's call for more political democracy in France. Apparently criticized by Stoffels for tending toward "immediate action," Tocqueville stressed the measured character of his approach and asked: "What do I want?"

He desired, he began, "not a republic, but a hereditary monarchy." More broadly, he added: "What I want is a central government energetic in its own sphere of action." But that central government needed to be limited by public opinion (popular will or sovereignty of the people), by the legislative power (separation and balance of power), and by provincial liberties (decentralization). "I think that a government of this kind can exist, and that, at the same time, the majority of the nation . . . can be involved in its own affairs, that political life can be spread almost everywhere, [and that] the direct or indirect exercise of political rights can be quite extensive" (referring to broad political rights and wide public participation).[34] The mention of extensive political rights and widespread political life recalled his discussions, especially in the 1835 *Democracy*, of towns, associations, and juries as free schools for liberty, where people participated in public life, learned about rights (their own and those of others) and the common good, and gained practical political experience.

The 1835 text presented the heart of his recommendations: "I think that if one does not come little by little to introduce and finally to found democratic institutions among us, and that if one renounces giving to all citizens ideas and sentiments that first prepare them for freedom and afterwards permit them the use of it, there will be independence for no one, neither for the bourgeois nor for the noble, nor for the poor man, nor for the rich man, but an equal tyranny for all."[35] Tocqueville's fundamental goals remained to instruct, to mold, and to prepare democratic society for liberty.

In yet another letter, written in 1840, Tocqueville explained the "political side" of his *Democracy* in different terms.

> Rest assured that the great peril of any democratic age is the destruction or excessive weakening of *the parts* of the social body as compared with *the whole*. Everything that reinforces the idea of the individual today is healthy. Everything that confers a separate existence on the species and enlarges the notion of the genus is dangerous. Contemporary thinking inclines naturally in this direction. In politics, the realist doctrine encourages all kinds of abuses of democracy. It facilitates despotism, centralization, contempt for individual rights, the doctrine of necessity, and the institutions and doctrines that permit the social body to trample on individuals and treat the nation as everything and the citizens as nothing.[36]

Here Tocqueville once again stressed the importance of respect for rights and especially those structures that counteract concentration of power by strengthening the *parts* against the *whole*; what he evidently had in mind were local liberties, associations, and any other mechanisms that supported individual independence and encouraged the groups, the potential centers of resistance to centralization, that elsewhere he called artificial "aristocratic persons." A central theme throughout the working papers and text of his *Democracy* remained the promotion of whatever tools that served to foster shared ideas, broad communication, and active contact among groups of citizens within the larger society. As always, Tocqueville wanted to use *free institutions* to shape the *habits of liberty.*

In drafts of his final chapter, he returned to the essential core of his politics and declared: "Use democracy to moderate democracy. That is the sole path of salvation that is open to us. Discern the sentiments, the ideas, the laws that, without being hostile to the principles of democracy, without being naturally incompatible with democracy, can however correct its unfortunate tendencies and, while modifying it, become incorporated with it. Beyond that everything is foolish and imprudent."[37] "Many men," he asserted in related papers, "consider democratic civil laws as an evil and democratic political laws as another and the greatest evil; but I say that the one is the sole remedy that you can apply to the other. All the idea of my politics is in this remark."[38]

In his book Tocqueville tried first to set forth the benefits and pitfalls of democracy and then to show readers how best to promote the former and avoid the latter. How best to safeguard liberty? In a nutshell, Tocqueville advised using democracy to heal itself. Only democracy could cure democracy. When, in the introduction to the first part of his work, he called for "a new political science . . . for a world altogether new," this basic recommendation helps to explain what he had in mind.[39]

7

What Are Some of Tocqueville's
Other Major Themes?

IF DEMOCRATIC DANGERS TO LIBERTY AND POSSIBLE REM-
edies in laws and mores constitute the heart of Tocqueville's message,
several other important themes remain for us to examine. Tocqueville's
economic views, as well as his understanding of the proper place and
function of government, deserve our attention. And Tocqueville, as we
will see, called himself a partisan of democracy. So we should also ask
why he endorsed democracy and how he answered the charges most
commonly made, especially by his own countrymen, against democracy.
Tocqueville's opinions about war also merit comment. Finally, Tocqueville, in both the 1835 and 1840 portions of his book, carefully described
the psychological effects of democracy. We therefore need to examine
his portrait of the democratic character. What, according to Tocqueville,
would the "new democratic man" be?

ECONOMICS AND THE ROLE OF GOVERNMENT

See in vol. 1 (1835): part 2, chap. 5, pp. 199–210, chap. 6, pp. 231–35, and chap. 10,
pp. 384–90; and in vol. 2 (1840): part 1, chaps. 8 and 14; part 2, chaps. 18, 19,
and 20; part 3, chaps. 6 and 7; and part 4, chap. 5.

We now come to two closely related topics. What does Tocqueville's *Democracy* reveal about his awareness of economic issues and his views
about the appropriate role of government in democratic societies?

Many readers have long assumed that Tocqueville was uninterested in
economic matters, knowing little and writing even less about such issues
in his book. As we have already noted, such a view is mistaken.[1] Dur-

ing his journey to America, Tocqueville recorded numerous conversations and reflections about economic developments, transportation and communication improvements, and technological changes in the United States. Although he visited such manufacturing cities as Pittsburgh and Cincinnati, he did miss the early industrialization of America, predicting instead a largely commercial future. This was a serious error.

But in his journey notes and in the pages of the 1835 *Democracy*, he addressed a variety of American economic topics. For example, he quickly saw and realized the significance of the widespread property holding and relatively high level of material comfort enjoyed by most Anglo-Americans. For Tocqueville the American example came to demonstrate that a healthy democracy required a rough economic equality and a basic level of physical well-being. Without these features, any democratic nation risked a serious gap between egalitarian assumptions, sentiments, and aspirations, on the one hand, and material realities, on the other.

Tocqueville also described the deeply commercial habits and industrial dynamism that characterized American society, commented on the rapid growth of American cities, noticed the proliferation and importance of the new commercial and industrial corporations, discussed both the effects of the division of labor and the American tendency to be jacks-of-all-trades, recognized the American fascination with speed, innovation, and planned obsolescence, and grasped the significance of the new steam technology and the impact of the transportation and communication transformation then underway on the future prosperity of the nation.

In one of the longer and most remarkable pieces in his journey notes, headed "Means of Increasing the Public Prosperity," Tocqueville marshaled proof from the United States to support his thesis that "the most infallible way to increase the prosperity of the nation is to encourage free communication among the people who inhabit it." In the essay he cited tangible evidence such as mail and newspaper circulation, roads, canals, railroads, steamboats, and the application of steam technology more generally. And he described the intangible but even more important characteristics of American mores, including energy and drive, an entrepreneurial spirit, a high level of education, and positive attitudes toward change and growth, including a strong expectation of constant improvement.[2]

These extended reflections on the causes of American economic success seemed to foreshadow a chapter in the 1835 portion of Tocqueville's book, to promise another case of carrying material from his journey notes directly into his text. But except for scattered comments about the dizzying pace of American economic and material development and his longer treatment of the commercial future of the United States, these remarks about American projects and attitudes remained buried in his travel diaries.

While still in the New World, Tocqueville also first mentioned in his travel diaries how the rise of manufacturing threatened to introduce new, unhealthy inequalities into democratic societies.[3] At least twice as he drafted the 1835 *Democracy*, he weighed the same danger. When describing the inexorable advance of equality, he cautioned: "however manufacturing." And in the working manuscript of his third chapter, "Social State of the Anglo-Americans," he wrote: "Put here, I think, the inequality arising from the accumulation of personal wealth of *manufacturing*." Perhaps most noteworthy is Tocqueville's realization as he wrote the 1840 part of his book that industrialization ranked with democracy as the two most significant forces at work in the world. "Equality is the great fact of our time. Industrial development, the second. Both augment the power of the government, or rather both are only one."[4]

These ideas were repeated and developed further in the 1840 *Democracy*, especially in one of Tocqueville's most famous chapters, "How Aristocracy Could Issue from Industry."[5] There and in several other chapters as well, he discussed the development of manufacturing; economic change (what has been called the market revolution); the rise of new industrial classes, especially the manufacturing aristocracy and the industrial working class; mass production and the economy of scale; the specialization or division of labor; the impact of democracy on wages, rents, and leases; and the link between liberty and commerce. Even more broadly, Tocqueville saw the way in which democracy favored commerce and industry and how it commercialized many (if not most) areas of society, including changing literature into a business and transforming citizens into consumers. He explored the connection between economic behavior and mores. And in his working papers and in the pages of his book, he presented a sharp critique of free enterprise without adequate social and moral constraints. His descriptions of the brutalization of the working class and his condemnation of unchecked capitalism as practiced by the industrial aristocracy are powerful pieces of economic and moral analysis. Tocqueville, in his *Democracy*, was no champion of unrestrained economic liberalism. Once again, Tocqueville as moralist comes to the fore.

But why did he not say more about economic matters in his book? What is said in the printed *Democracy* about economics was shaped not so much by blindness as by choice. In his drafts, as well as in the published text, Tocqueville presented some of the reasons for his intellectual choices. He explained that, although he was aware of other dimensions of a particular issue, he sometimes decided very consciously to focus on the dimension he most wanted to address and to set the other dimensions aside. In the foreword of the 1840 *Democracy* he wrote:

> I must warn the reader right away against an error that would be very prejudicial to me. In seeing me attribute so many diverse effects to equality, he could conclude that I consider equality to be the unique cause of all that happens in our day. That would be to suppose that I had a very narrow view. There are a host of opinions, sentiments, and instincts in our time that owe their birth to facts alien or even contrary to equality. . . . I recognize the existence of all these different causes and their power, but to speak of them is not my subject. I have not undertaken to show the reason for all our penchants and ideas; I only wanted to bring out the extent to which equality has modified the one and the other.[6]

This kind of decision marked *Democracy* in important ways, including how Tocqueville addressed economic matters. It reaffirms the judgment that some of the silences (or near silences) of *Democracy* do not betray blind spots or lack of awareness, but rather Tocqueville's choices about what he preferred to address, what was closest to his heart and to his most personal moral and philosophical beliefs, and what he decided to leave to others. Tocqueville realized that he could not write about all of the major features of modern society that he recognized. He decided to write a "philosophico-political" work[7] and to concentrate on analyzing *democracy*. He knew, for example, that industrialization was the other great force at work in the modern world, but he chose to leave the full elaboration of that theme to others.

Although, especially in his travel diaries, Tocqueville presented a perceptive analysis of economic attitudes and developments in the American republic, the United States did not provide the primary inspiration for his economic ideas. His major sources were found elsewhere. Crossing the Atlantic, Tocqueville read Jean-Baptiste Say, a political economist who discussed, among other topics, the division of labor. In 1833, in England, Tocqueville first met another prominent political economist, Nassau William Senior; the two men subsequently maintained a long connection and correspondence. And as he drafted the 1835 *Democracy*, he was also preparing an essay on poverty, "Memoir on Pauperism." For that paper he read a work by Alban de Villeneuve-Bargemont, yet another political economist, who specifically described the rise of a new manufacturing aristocracy and presented a strong moral critique of unrestrained capitalism. Probably even more important for Tocqueville's 1840 *Democracy* was his second journey to England in 1835, after the publication of the first portion of his book. During his first visit in 1833, he had visited no manufacturing centers. But in 1835 he went to Manchester and was shocked by what he saw; the "dark satanic mills" seemed to confirm all that Villeneuve-Bargemont had said. So Tocqueville's views on economic matters stand as a good example of the diversity of his sources, readings, and experiences as he thought and wrote.

A S WE ALREADY KNOW, ALTHOUGH TOCQUEVILLE WARNED against the new democratic despotism of the tutelary state, he did not oppose centralized power or active government as such; great national enterprises, he believed, required a strong and active central power.[8] Tocqueville's message is quite consistent throughout the writing of his *Democracy*.

He had noticed that in the United States major economic undertakings were often shared enterprises. In his travel diaries he declared:

In Europe it is generally believed that the leading maxim of government in America is *laisser faire*: that the government is purely a spectator, observing the progress of society which is driven by individual self-interest. This is a mistake. True, the American government does not involve itself in everything, as ours does. It does not seek to anticipate all needs and do whatever needs to be done. It distributes no bonuses, does not encourage commerce, and does not act as patron to arts and letters. But when it comes to projects of great public utility, it seldom leaves the job to private individuals, but acts on its own. . . . Note however that there are no rules. Companies, towns and private individuals cooperate with the state in a myriad of ways. . . . There is no exclusive system here. America eschews the uniformity of system that certain superficial and metaphysical minds find so appealing of late. On the contrary, difference and variety are the watchwords of American institutions, laws, government, and everyday life.[9]

Tocqueville realized that the preferred American method for accomplishing "internal improvements" was to blend private and governmental (local, state, and federal) support. The American system avoided both the risk that most (or all) major economic developments would be entirely in private hands, an approach that presented the danger of the industrial aristocracy, and the threat that most (or all) major undertakings would be done by the government; the latter was the French model of the late 1830s that Tocqueville opposed as leading to administrative centralization and bureaucratic despotism. The Americans, Tocqueville realized, had discovered a mixed system that balanced public and private participation, public and private responsibility. This blended approach allowed the Americans to accomplish wonders. For France, he argued that if the administration became deeply involved in great industrial enterprises, it had to be checked by the legislature and by the courts. If the state acted alone, liberty was in danger.[10]

In the 1835 *Democracy* he treated this topic only tangentially, simply noting the advantages of the American mixed approach. "Since the action of individual forces is joined to the action of social forces, they [the Americans] often succeed in doing what the most concentrated and most energetic administration would be in no condition to execute."[11] As the

1840 *Democracy* took shape, however, Tocqueville drafted two brief fragments on the role of government in democratic societies.

The first, on the general topic of education, urged governments in democracies to support and fund learned academies for the arts and sciences in order to foster cultural and scientific work, especially research and learning in the theoretical sciences. Under the heading "Of Academic Institutions under Democracy," he declared: "An academy having the goal of making the men who apply themselves to the arts or to the sciences famous and giving them, at State expense, the comfort and leisure that the democratic social state often denies to them, is an institution that can be not to the taste of a democratic nation, but one that is never contrary to and can sometimes be necessary to the existence of a democracy. It is an eminently democratic institution." He then added: "Of the need for paid learned bodies in democracies. This need increases as peoples turn towards democracy. This truth understood with difficulty by the democracy. Opposite natural inclination that you must combat. The Americans give way to it."[12]

The second, titled "Of the Manner in Which American Governments Act toward Associations," described the different ways in which the English and American governments treated corporations (economic associations). The former followed a course of action appropriate to aristocracies, leaving major efforts in private hands; the latter pursued a policy better suited to promoting prosperity and economic development in democracies. "In England, the State mingles strictly only in its own affairs. Often it even relies on individuals for the task of undertaking and completing works whose usefulness or grandeur have an almost national appearance. . . . It often happens that [the Americans] lend to certain associations the support of the State or even charge the State with taking their place. There are works that do not precisely have a national character, but whose execution is very difficult, in which the government takes part in the United States, or that it carries out at its expense."[13]

Elsewhere in drafts of the 1840 portion of his book, Tocqueville called upon the government to regulate private commercial and industrial corporations.[14] In all three of these cases, for a variety of reasons that he explained in his working papers, Tocqueville decided not to include his remarks in his text. But, as these fragments show, he should not be read as an advocate of the least possible government. The real question, according to Tocqueville, was not whether or not the state should participate, but where and how to draw the limits of state participation. No involvement endangered national prosperity and progress. Too much involvement threatened liberty and risked bureaucratic despotism. We also need to recognize that during the long consideration of this issue that appears in the working papers of the 1840 *Democracy*, Tocqueville frequently cited contemporary French issues and recounted public debates and even private conversations about the appropriate role of government in French economic and industrial projects of the period. Here we can see how deeply France and French affairs influenced the writing of Tocqueville's book, especially the final section of the 1840 portion.

For him, the issue was one of balance between private and public prerogatives. In the 1840 text he declared: "It is at once necessary and desirable that the central power that directs a democratic people be active and powerful. There is no question of rendering it weak or indolent, but only of preventing it from abusing its agility and force."[15] "Among democratic nations," he observed in his drafts,

> . . . the State must be involved in more *enterprises* than in others. Nuance to observe in that. If the State itself takes charge of everything, it finishes by throwing individuals into nothingness. [This was the tendency of the French system.] . . . Nuances very delicate, difficult to grasp. Position that is very easy to abuse. English system of not getting involved in anything. Aristocratic system. Liberty gives the desire and the idea of doing great things, and individuals powerful enough to do them easily by associating. American system in which the State encourages and does not share in the activities of enterprises, loans money, grants land, does nothing by itself."[16]

Tocqueville urged France to follow at least some version of the middle way, modeled on America. Once again it was a question of "sorting out the limits of the pairs."

So Tocqueville was not a spokesman for completely unregulated capitalism, nor did he argue for the least possible government. In both cases he characteristically sought the middle ground, searching for ways both to avoid the economic, social and moral abuses of unchecked capitalism, and to find the appropriate role for government in great national projects necessary for the public good.[17]

A PARTISAN OF DEMOCRACY?

See in vol. 1 (1835): part 2, chap. 5; chap. 6, pp. 231–35; chap. 7, pp. 238–39 and 246–48; and chap. 9, pp. 298–302; and in vol. 2 (1840): part 2, chap. 1; part 4, chaps. 1 and 8.

Reading Tocqueville's *Democracy in America* leaves a nagging question unanswered. Where did Tocqueville stand on democracy? The habitual effort in his book to remain neutral, to avoid becoming a party man, left his position unclear. We know that he saw advancing democracy as inevitable and providential. And we are aware that he wrote his work largely to show the benefits and disadvantages of democracy, and then to suggest how to enhance the first and avoid the second. Tocqueville also wanted to reconcile his countrymen (and other readers) to an inescapable democratic future and to promote the development of a democratic France that remained free and stable. But did he actually favor democracy?

As we have noted, among major democratic dangers and threats to liberty, he included materialism, individualism, and the concentration of power. Throughout his *Democracy* Tocqueville also pointed to other more miscellaneous, but still significant flaws. In each case, the American republic served as the not very happy example. From what he had witnessed in the New World, Tocqueville concluded that democracy bred instability in specific laws and administrative policies, mediocrity in political leadership, inability to conduct complex foreign affairs, and, because of the constant need to flatter the people, a general debasement of the public discourse.

Despite these grave challenges to liberty and other serious democratic weaknesses, however, Tocqueville in the working papers of his book took a positive stance toward democracy. "You see that my tendencies are always democratic. I am a partisan of democracy without having any illusion about its faults and without failing to recognize its dangers."[18] In this view, he never wavered. Tocqueville not only worried about how democracy menaced liberty (an argument widely recognized by readers), but also praised the way in which democracy engendered a love of liberty, a taste for free institutions, and a propensity for political independence (a counterargument often overlooked).[19]

After the publication of the 1835 *Democracy*, Tocqueville wrote to John Stuart Mill, thanking him for his complimentary and perceptive review and admitting: "I love liberty by taste, equality by instinct and reason. These two passions, which so many pretend to have, I am convinced that I really feel in myself." In the letter he compared French and English friends of democracy, identifying himself as more of an English democrat, whose "final object seems to me to be, in reality, to put the majority of citizens in a fit state of governing and to make it capable of governing. Faithful to their principles, they do not claim to force the people to be happy in the way that they judge most suitable, but they want to see to it that the people are in a fit state to discern it, and discerning it, to conform to it."

He concluded: "I am myself a democrat in this sense. . . . You know that I am not exaggerating the final result of the great Democratic Revolution that is taking place at this moment in the world; I do not regard it in the same light as the Israelites saw the Promised Land. But, on the whole, I believe it to be useful and necessary, and work toward it resolutely, without hesitation, without enthusiasm, and, I hope, without weakness."[20] Although in this letter Tocqueville claimed a love of equality by instinct, the main message of the epistle is an attachment by reason. He identified as a partisan of democracy mostly by reasoned judgment; the democratic revolution was "useful and necessary." His willingness to speak for democracy was a matter more of the mind than of the heart.

In yet another letter written just after the publication of the 1835 *Democracy*, Tocqueville explained his strategy to Eugène Stoffels. He wanted those with an idealized dream of democracy to recognize the necessity of "certain conditions of enlightenment, of private morality, of beliefs." "To men for whom the word *democracy* is synonymous with upheaval, anarchy, spoliation, murders, I tried to show that democracy could manage to govern society while respecting fortunes, recognizing rights, securing liberty, honoring beliefs; that if democratic government developed less than some other governments certain beautiful faculties of the human soul, it had beautiful and grand sides; and that perhaps, after all, the will of God was to diffuse a mediocre happiness on the totality of men, and not to concentrate a large amount of felicity on some and allow only a small number to approach perfection."[21]

Three elements in this statement stand out: Tocqueville's appeal, once again, to the will of God to validate the democratic revolution; his presumption that a widespread middling happiness was preferable to extreme inequalities of opportunity for "felicity" and "perfection"; and his insistence that democracy had its "beautiful and grand sides." In his remarks he also offered both a thumbnail sketch of common accusations against democracy and his summarized replies.

Tocqueville expressed this measured support for democracy in veiled ways in both parts of his work. Perhaps he came closest to disclosing his views as a partisan of democracy in two places in his text, first, in 1835, in the subsection entitled "Importance of What Precedes in Relation to Europe." The second instance, in 1840, appeared in the final chapter of his work.[22] Although the latter chapter is largely rhetorical, designed to be an eloquent summation, Tocqueville did reveal his complex reactions to the emerging democratic world, ultimately equating democracy once again with divine purpose.

He began negatively, echoing the views of many of his fellow citizens.

If among all these diverse features I seek the one that appears to me the most general and the most striking, I come to see that what may be remarked in fortunes is represented in a thousand other forms. Almost all extremes become milder and softer; almost all prominent points are worn down to make a place for something middling that is at once less high and less low, less brilliant and less obscure than what used to be seen in the world. I let my regard wander over this innumerable crowd composed of similar beings, in which nothing is elevated and nothing lowered. The spectacle of this universal uniformity saddens and chills me, and I am tempted to regret the society that is no longer.[23]

But his argument then took a different turn.

> When the world was filled with very great and very small men, very rich
> and very poor, very learned and very ignorant, I turned my regard away
> from the second and attached it only to the first, and these delighted my
> view. . . . It is not the same with the all-powerful and eternal Being, whose
> eye necessarily envelops the sum of things and who sees distinctly, though
> at once, the whole human race and each man. It is natural to believe that
> what most satisfies the regard of this creator and preserver of men is not
> the singular prosperity of some, but the greatest well-being of all; what
> seems to me decadence is therefore progress in his eyes; what wounds me,
> is agreeable to him. Equality is perhaps less elevated; but it is more just,
> and its justice makes for its greatness and its beauty. I strive to enter into
> this point of view of God, and it is from there that I seek to consider and
> judge human things.[24]

Here was no ringing affirmation of the democratic revolution, but once again Tocqueville granted the justice, grandeur, and beauty of democracy.

So *Democracy in America*, especially the 1840 portion, may be read as an extended defense of democracy, an almost point-by-point refutation of some of the most common complaints made against it, especially by Tocqueville's fellow Frenchmen. (And perhaps he was attempting to answer his own fears as well.) From this perspective, Tocqueville's work may be understood as a long exercise in reassurance. As Tocqueville treated successive topics, he argued that democracy changes the character of all of society, giving everything a new twist. Democracy, he asserted, brought not destruction, but transformation. Here again was one of the central messages of his book.

Democracy and Religion

For references see previous segment on religion.

Critics commonly viewed democracy as incompatible with religion. Tocqueville, as we have already observed, cited the American example in both parts of his work to demonstrate, in reply, how democracy and faith, liberty and religion, could merge and strengthen each other.

Democracy and Intellectual Creativity

See in vol. 1 (1835): part 2, chap. 7, pp. 243–45; and in vol. 2 (1840): part 1, chaps. 9 and 10; part 3, chap. 21.

As part of the broad challenge to democratic laws and institutions, many of Tocqueville's contemporaries in France asked whether democracy posed a risk to intellectual independence, freedom of thought, and high cultural achievement. Tocqueville's discussion of the power of the majority over thought and opinion demonstrates that he too worried whether advancing equality endangered civilization itself. Would the pressure of public opinion on new or different ideas cause "the human mind to stop"?

Tocqueville faced the issue directly while still traveling in the New World. "Why, when civilization spreads, does the number of prominent men decrease? Why, when knowledge becomes the province of all, does great intellectual talent become more rare? Why, when there is no longer a lower class, is there no longer an upper class either? . . . America clearly raises these questions. But who can answer them?"[25] Did democracy undermine intellectual excellence and cultural achievement? As Tocqueville wrote the 1835 *Democracy*, he provided an initial answer. His chapter on the omnipotence of the majority included the premise that the United States simply lacked a vibrant higher culture.[26]

In the 1840 *Democracy*, in his chapter on the aptitude and taste for the sciences, literature, and the arts among democratic peoples, Tocqueville repeated the same critical comments about cultural achievement in the United States, but refused to accept the American example as proof that democracy led to barbarism.

> One must recognize that among the civilized peoples of our day there are few in whom the advanced sciences have made less progress than in the United States, and who have furnished fewer great artists, illustrious poets and celebrated writers. Several Europeans, struck by this spectacle, have considered it a natural and inevitable result of equality, and they have thought that, if a democratic social state and institutions once came to prevail over all the earth, the human mind would see the lights that en-

lighten it gradually dimmed, and men would fall back into darkness. Those who reason thus, I think, confuse several ideas that it would be important to divide and examine separately. Without wishing to, they mix what is democratic with what is only American."[27]

"The situation of the Americans is . . . entirely exceptional," he concluded. ". . . Let us therefore cease to see all democratic nations in the shape of the American people and try finally to view them with their own features."[28]

Once again Tocqueville insisted on American singularity and argued that the United States proved nothing about the influence of democracy on civilization. After carefully explaining the reasons why the American situation was exceptional, he returned in his working manuscript to the larger issue. "I take the European peoples such as they appear to my eyes with their ancient traditions, their acquired enlightenment, their liberties, and I wonder if by becoming democratic they run the risk of falling back into a sort of barbarism."[29]

In the chapter he presented a direct refutation of this common charge against democracy. Expanding equality, he argued, would unlock a restless ambition in cultural pursuits and would also greatly increase "the number of those who cultivate the sciences, letters, and arts."[30] Instead of discouraging intellectual and cultural achievement, democracy would stimulate it. "A prodigious activity [would be] awakened in the world of the intellect."[31]

"It is therefore not true," he asserted in the 1840 text, "to say that men who live in democratic centuries are naturally indifferent to the sciences, letters, and arts; one must only recognize that they cultivate them in their own manner."[32] According to Tocqueville, at least in this chapter of his book, democracy would lead not to barbarism, but to a different sort of cultural flowering.

Tocqueville had not finished his consideration of the issue, however. If his position in one chapter of the 1840 *Democracy* was more hopeful, his conclusion in others remained ambiguous, even negative. We have already noted the language in his portrait of the new democratic despotism; the tutelary state covers the surface of society "with a network of small, complicated, painstaking, uniform rules through which the most original minds . . . cannot clear a way."[33] So democracy, without liberty, would suffocate new ideas.

In the chapter entitled "Why Great Revolutions Will Become Rare," Tocqueville also addressed the question of intellectual innovation. The complaint that democracy led to social and political instability and to revolution and anarchy was commonly made in France. Tocqueville's primary purpose in his chapter was to refute that charge and instead to raise the contrasting specter of immobility and stagnation in democratic nations. "This idea that the democratic social state is anti-revolutionary," he observed in a rough draft, "so shocks accepted ideas that I must win over the mind of the reader little by little, and for that I must begin by saying that this social state is less *revolutionary* than is supposed. I begin there and by an imperceptible curve I arrive at saying that there is room to fear that it is not revolutionary enough. True idea, but which would seem paradoxical at first view."[34] In a page enclosed with his working manuscript, he admitted: "But I want to aim still further and I am going even as far as imagining that the final result of democracy will be to make the human mind too immobile and human opinions too stable."[35]

Tocqueville argued in his chapter that important intellectual innovations, like great political revolutions, would become rare in democratic societies. His 1840 text concluded:

> I cannot prevent myself from fearing that men will arrive at the point of looking on every new theory as a peril, every innovation as a distressing trouble, every social progress as a first step toward a revolution, and that they will altogether refuse to move for fear that they will be carried away. . . . People believe that the new societies are going to change face daily, and I am afraid that in the end they will be too unchangeably fixed in the same institutions, the same prejudices, the same mores, so that the human race will stop and limit itself; that the mind will fold and refold . . . around itself eternally without producing new ideas, that man will exhaust himself in small, solitary, sterile motions, and that, while constantly moving, humanity will no longer advance.[36]

Here Tocqueville offered his readers a portrait of intellectual and cultural stagnation nearly as grim as that of the shepherd state.

Tocqueville's long reflection, at least from 1831 to 1840, on whether democracy would lead to a new barbarism beautifully illustrates one of the fundamental traits of his thought: constant reconsideration. As he wrote, he continued to revisit a question in his mind, focusing in turn on different dimensions of the issue, often amending previous conclusions, and sometimes settling on apparently opposing answers. This characteristic of his thinking and writing should make us cautious about taking Tocqueville's positions too absolutely. Complexity and subtlety are hallmarks of the message of *Democracy in America*.

Why does Tocqueville in his *Democracy* offer such conflicting visions about cultural and intellectual vitality in democratic nations? The difference between a fundamental change in the mental framework of a society, such as the Reformation (to repeat Tocqueville's example), and ongoing creativity in the sciences, arts, and letters partially explains his contrasting conclusions. But a careful reading of his arguments demonstrates the key role played by free institutions, such as local liberties, associations, and a free press, in shaping and reconciling his conclusions. On the one hand, if democratic societies allowed individuals to be in contact with each other, to express, hear, and support new ideas and opinions, then cultural and intellectual development remained not only possible, but also probable. On the other hand, if democracy came without freedom, then stagnation would settle in. Here, once again, Tocqueville's *Democracy* made an eloquent case for liberty.

Democracy and Morality

See in vol. 2 (1840): part 3, chaps. 1, 8–12, and 18.

Democracy, some critics also claimed, meant a breakdown in basic morality. Tocqueville addressed part of this concern in his excellent 1840 chapter on honor, in which he argued that democracy, despite the fears of some, does not eradicate honor and moral laws, but instead brings about a new kind of honor: "simple and general notions of good and evil."[37]

But the most common fear about democracy and morals centered on the family and on traditional relationships between men and women, including marriage. In his book Tocqueville admitted that, in democratic societies, family relationships would be modified, but insisted, in a remarkable series of chapters, that the changes would be for the better. Much of his argument was grounded once again in what he had seen in the New World, but for some parts of his discussion, he relied instead on what he observed around him among families in France.

In his travel diaries, in his letters home, and in the 1835 portion of his work, Tocqueville marveled at the chaste morals of the Americans, their respect for the conjugal bond, and the role of American women as those who shaped morals in the society. He also noticed and admired the strength and resilience of the American pioneer wife. By 1840, his treatment broadened into a fuller consideration of the impact of democracy on the family, on morals, on American women, and on the relationship between the genders. Within the family, he asserted, democracy reduced the formal distances between father and sons and among brothers. If democracy loosened social bonds, tending to isolate individuals, it tightened natural ones, leading to more intimate, more affectionate, and milder familial ties. Tocqueville pointed out that the "sweet pleasures" of this transformation captivated even traditional aristocratic families in France, modifying their domestic mores as well.[38]

The core of his response to the detractors of democracy, however, involved his insistence on the purity and regularity of morals, on marital fidelity, and on what he saw as the sound relationship between men and women in the United States. American young women—educated, honest, independent (even bold), but virtuous—found their marriage partners by preference, and then, again by choice, gave up their youthful independence to enter, as a wife, into a "small circle of interests and domestic duties."[39] For them, according to Tocqueville, marriage was a kind of self-imposed cloister. For Tocqueville, marriage by inclination, rather than by paternal or social dictate, demonstrated how democracy promoted milder mores, including familial and marital affection. Marriage also served, for him, as a key measure of advancing equality. A democratic social state made marriage by mutual attraction and between social classes possible. For a French aristocrat with an English middle-class wife, this was a very personal message.

Tocqueville specifically tried to answer the expectation, among some enemies of democracy, that equality would obscure distinctions between the sexes, dissolve the traditional roles of men and women, and lead ultimately to moral and sexual anarchy. To combat this view, he not only described the American wife and marriage, but also carefully explained how Americans understood the emancipation of women. In the New World republic, equality for women meant neither free love nor the end of acknowledged differences between men and women. In America, he wrote, women were seen as equal to, but not the same as men; a strict division of functions was maintained. Women lived in a separate domestic world, leaving public roles to men. For Tocqueville, this doctrine of separate spheres reflected the natural and biological differences between the sexes. He famously concluded his analysis with high praise for American women. "[If] one asked me to what do I think one must principally attribute the singular prosperity and growing force of [the American] people, I would answer that it is to the superiority of its women."[40]

Tocqueville perceptively grasped the development of distinctive social spheres for men and women in early nineteenth-century America, the kind of separate, but (supposedly) equal status that arose between the sexes in that period. But his discussion contained serious flaws. His compliments aside, his chapters essentially asserted the inherent inferiority of women. His remarks papered over the profound inequalities facing women, made the separation of women from public life into a female choice, and, in silence and without acknowledgment, focused almost entirely on white, or Anglo-American, middle-class women, especially those in the northern cities of the United States. Although the chapters recognized the education of American women, they also missed the rapidly developing engagement of those women in reform and other activities outside the domestic sphere. In short, Tocqueville's analysis exposes some of his more serious errors and reveals a good deal about his own gender prejudices. Nonetheless, his chapters made his essential point; democracy, he believed, was favorable to good morals. The faultfinders were wrong.

Democracy and Revolution

See in vol. 1 (1835): part 2, chap. 10, pp. 379–84; and in vol. 2 (1840):
part 3, chaps. 17 and 21.

Yet another charge against democracy was the presumed connection between democracy and revolution. As Tocqueville wrote in the letter to
Stoffels cited above, in the thinking of many of his contemporaries, democracy meant profound political and social instability, "upheaval, anarchy, spoliation, murders." If Tocqueville reached the American shore also
suspecting that democracy foreshadowed revolution, the United States
taught him otherwise. In the New World republic he saw democrats who
were emphatically not revolutionary, except in their impact on the material world. He realized that beneath the constant surface commotion of
America there existed a nearly unchanging bedrock of principles and assumptions, of mores. The Americans were profoundly antirevolutionary,
in any social or political sense. So democracy did not mean revolution.
For Tocqueville this too was an American discovery. Democracy, as he
would write in the 1840 portion of his book, in fact worked against great
social and political revolutions. Here was a conclusion specifically designed to assuage the fears of his countrymen.

One of Tocqueville's abiding challenges, as he recognized, was to separate what was American from what was democratic. He faced the same
critical need to make distinctions again when he considered democracy
and revolution.

> Idea to bring very much forward. . . . Effects of democracy and particularly
> harmful effects that are exaggerated in the period of revolution when the
> democratic social state, mores and laws become established. . . . The great
> difficulty in the study of democracy is to distinguish what is democratic
> from what is only revolutionary. This is very difficult because examples are
> lacking. There is no European people among whom democracy has settled
> down, and America is in an exceptional situation. The state of literature
> in France is not only democratic, but revolutionary. Public morality, id.
> Religious opinions, id. Political opinions, id.[41]

In the introduction to the 1835 *Democracy*, Tocqueville combined images of advancing democracy and revolution and wrote about a great democratic revolution. But he also realized that the bitter revolutionary struggle in France and Europe made it hard to separate what resulted from democracy and what resulted from profound social and political conflict.[42] America, he famously, if erroneously, observed, enjoyed democracy without having undergone a revolution. France and Europe, on the other hand, could not escape the passions spawned by revolution, the intense emotions that Tocqueville in his book labeled the *revolutionary spirit*.

"There are," he declared in his 1840 text, "certain habits, certain ideas, and certain vices that are proper to a state of revolution. . . . [One] becomes attached to the principle of social utility, one creates the dogma of political necessity, and one willingly becomes accustomed to sacrificing particular interests without scruple and to riding roughshod over individual rights in order to attain more promptly the general end that one proposes."[43] Such attitudes were especially dangerous in democracies, where they threatened to take root and become pervasive and permanent.

So in his *Democracy* Tocqueville undertook the dual task of treating democracy and revolution as two forces simultaneously at work in the world and then of identifying their distinctive features. Especially in the 1840 portion, revolution and the revolutionary spirit, which Tocqueville saw as the destructive and enduring consequence of revolution, helped to explain why the French and American cases differed so greatly. As we noticed earlier, the contrast between the two countries arose not only out of the gap in France between social democracy and political democracy, between mores and laws. In Tocqueville's view, democracy in France was also profoundly contaminated by a revolutionary spirit that worsened many of the weaknesses and disadvantages of democracy. He attempted to persuade his readers that the American republic—supposedly revolution-free—served as a better illustration of the potential of democracy. Especially to understand the possible benefits of democracy, he urged, cast your eyes not on a diseased France, but on a healthy America.

DEMOCRACY AND WAR

In vol. 2 (1840): part 2, chap. 17; part 3, chap. 22.

According to Tocqueville, democracy focused attention on narrow private interests (individualism) and the good things of the earth (materialism). It therefore threatened to weaken souls, to loosen the springs of action, and to divert human beings from higher nonmaterial aspirations and efforts. Tocqueville worried about the rise of an apathetic mass constantly spinning around itself, pursuing its petty desires and becoming incapable of any lofty endeavors. We have already mentioned these moral dangers of democracy. What did Tocqueville propose to do about them? How to enlarge and energize souls? How to spiritualize human beings and elevate their gaze above the level of small, material concerns? Part of Tocqueville's response is already clear. To lift men out of themselves and to promote wider connections and higher purposes, he advocated religion and the various free schools of liberty, especially associations and local liberties. But we need to acknowledge that sometimes he had yet another solution in mind.

Tocqueville was a patriot, committed to the greatness, cultural leadership and civilizing mission of France. He assumed that France, with its distinctive values, was the beacon of European civilization, lighting the way to the highest social and political ideals. In his letters home from America, travel notes and book, he severely criticized and even mocked the Americans for their national pride and extreme patriotic sensitivity, but seemed not to see the same traits in himself.

We have already noticed that, for Tocqueville, war posed a special danger to liberty for democratic nations. It heightened the risk of centralization and threatened, in particular, to usher in the military tyrant, or at least to gather all power into the hands of the executive power. It foreshadowed the new despotism of the clerk and the soldier. But his vision of France as a great nation perhaps helps to explain a contrary assessment of war also found in *Democracy in America*. In his work Tocqueville described and even recommended war and, by implication, great national ventures as cures for the democratic maladies of petty materialism, individualism, and public apathy—what he called the fruit of individualism.[44]

In the 1840 portion of his book he wrote: "I do not wish to speak ill of war; war almost always enlarges the thought of a people and elevates its heart. There are cases where only it can arrest the excessive development of certain penchants that equality naturally gives rise to, and where, for certain deep-seated maladies to which democratic societies are subject, it must be considered almost necessary. War has great advantages. . . ."[45]

In 1837, as he drafted the second half of his book, Tocqueville also wrote his first articles on Algeria, praising French colonization as the legitimate civilizing mission of a great nation. And much of his political career and private correspondence after 1840 would continue to reflect a hypersensitive nationalism and even an occasionally bellicose attitude. So once again we are confronted by contrary messages from Tocqueville's book. On the one hand, he warned against war for promoting centralization and despotism. On the other, he praised war for countering democratic ills. And once again, he failed to reconcile these opposite views for his readers.[46]

THE DEMOCRATIC CHARACTER

See in vol. 1 (1835): part 1, chap. 2, pp. 27–29; part 2, chap. 5, pp. 187–90 and 212–20; chap. 9, pp. 265–74; and in vol. 2 (1840): part 1, chap. 8; part 2, chaps. 11, 13, and 17.

One of the most brilliant and original dimensions of Tocqueville's book is his effort to trace how democracy refashioned human psychology. In this endeavor, he played not the philosopher, historian, political theorist, political economist, or even the moralist, but the psychologist or social psychologist. He believed that the emerging democratic society would call forth a new creature: a "democratic man," marked by particular mores and exhibiting a characteristic set of attitudes, beliefs, habits, and ideas. In various chapters, especially in the 1840 portion of his work, he attempted to sketch this new democratic psychology for readers.

The story of his effort begins, however, with his developing description of the American national character. From the first days of his journey, he observed the behavior and attitudes of those around him and began to assemble the basic elements of a full portrait. Throughout the writing of his book, as we have noted, the concepts of national character, race, and even mores remained somewhat vague and elusive in Tocqueville's thinking. In an early version of his working manuscript, however, he presented a tentative definition of national character. "There is indeed in the bent of the ideas and tastes of a people a hidden force that struggles with advantage against revolutions and time. This intellectual physiognomy of nations, which is called their character, is found throughout all the centuries of their history and amid the innumerable changes that take place in the social state, beliefs and laws. A strange thing! What is least perceptible and most difficult to define among a people is at the same time what you find most enduring among them."[47]

This working definition largely overlapped what Tocqueville meant by mores. So his search for the American national character was essentially an exploration of the mores of a particular nation. In his travel diaries and in the working papers and text of his book, Tocqueville attempted to depict the "bent of the ideas and tastes," the "intellectual physiognomy" of the Americans. He eventually assembled a long list of traits, both positive and negative, a few of which we have already examined. Because many of these features were specific to the citizens of the New World republic, Tocqueville would not ultimately apply all of them to democratic peoples in general. Some, however, became crucial elements of the new democratic psychology, as described by Tocqueville in 1840.

As we observed, Tocqueville, in the pages of his 1840 work, broadened the American passion for material well-being into a characteristic of all democratic peoples. Such a wider application, we know, marked a shift away from America as Tocqueville drafted the last portion of his book. His task evolved from describing the American national character to portraying democratic mores in general and democratic psychology in particular.

Tocqueville acknowledged this modified goal in a draft of the foreword to his 1840 volumes.

The work which appears at this moment . . . is not an entirely new work. It is the second and last part of a book that I published five years ago on democracy in the United States. . . . [The men who live in a democratic social state] naturally adopt certain laws, and contract certain habits of government that are appropriate to them. This same equality and these same causes influence not only their political ideas and habits, but also all their habits and all their ideas. [They] conceive new opinions; they adopt new mores; they establish relationships among themselves that did not exist or modify those that already existed. The appearance of civil society is not less changed than the physiognomy of the political world. The object of the book that I published five years ago was to show the first effects of equality; this one wants to depict the second. The two parts united form a single whole."[48]

Here we can only present a cursory list of the most essential traits of the new democratic mores as described by Tocqueville. Some have already been noted. Democratic people exhibited or felt a passion for material well-being (materialism); a love of equality; an assumption of being equal to others and an expectation of being treated as an equal (the sentiment of equality); a sense of isolation and a tendency to turn inward to the private sphere of family and friends (individualism); a desire for change, at least on superficial levels, and an assumption of constant improvement;[49] and an easy yielding to momentary emotions and a lack of sustained attention.[50]

Other characteristics were more clearly psychological. People in democratic societies, according to Tocqueville, were consumed by envy,[51] by anxiety and insecurity (about both status and material well-being),[52] by chronic frustration and discontent (about an always elusive equality and a lack of time to achieve material desires),[53] and finally by a profound restlessness.[54]

Note how these democratic mores and psychological traits, on the one hand, reinforce the democratic dangers that so worried Tocqueville, and, on the other, present in themselves yet another major menace in democratic societies. "Democratic man," as envisioned by Tocqueville, often behaved and reacted in ways that were neither attractive, nor admirable, nor healthy in the long run. This psychological sketch of the democratic character in 1840 closely mirrored Tocqueville's description of the Anglo-American between 1831 and 1835. But as we noted earlier when discussing democratic materialism, it was inspired as well both by Tocqueville's preexisting critical stance toward middle-class mores, as he understood them, and by his alarm about the developing attitudes and behavior of his countrymen in France of the 1830s.

Whatever the combination of sources, Tocqueville's portrait of democratic psychology is remarkably negative and once again illustrates his ambivalence about the coming of democracy.

TOCQUEVILLE'S MAJOR THEMES RECONSIDERED

We began our consideration of Tocqueville's major themes by recognizing that such a survey could be organized in a variety of ways. Now, having completed our review, we can revisit this question and consider some of these competing approaches. Of course, no single organizing principle is definitive. Each one has strengths and weaknesses; each throws a different light on Tocqueville's thinking and writing; but each can be useful for introducing readers to his most fundamental ideas and questions.

Democracy in America can be understood as a study in contrasting pairs, such as aristocracy and democracy, equality and liberty, liberty and despotism, mores and laws, habits and art, or revolution and democracy. Closely related to these broader dualisms is Tocqueville's habit of setting America against France, a healthy against an unhealthy democracy, or even America as the model republic (the idealized image) against America as the example of excessive democracy (the warning image). As a way to explore Tocqueville's book, this intellectual technique can even be expanded, as Tocqueville himself did, to tripartite contrasts and comparisons, notably America, France, and England; or democracy, a fixed aristocracy (or caste), and an open aristocracy.

Another possible path to understanding is to trace systematically how democracy influences each area of society: social, political, legal, cultural, religious, economic, intellectual, psychological, moral, and so on. Or an analysis could simply focus on a thorough exploration of Tocqueville's three major causes: mores, laws, and circumstances, examining what each means and how each shapes any given society. Still another broad approach, as we have just seen, is to look at Tocqueville's depiction of the new democratic man. A full portrait of the psychology and character, the mind and emotions, the fears and hopes of human beings in the age of democracy would eventually lead readers into almost all of the twists and turns of Tocqueville's thinking. Grappling with *Democracy in America* in any of these deceptively simple ways would nonetheless quickly get into the core of Tocqueville's book.

Yet another perspective would emerge from an elaborate definition of key terms, including equality, democracy, liberty, social state, laws, mores, circumstances, point of departure, American federalism, tyranny of the majority, individualism, revolutionary spirit, national character, and the new democratic despotism. This option would parallel Tocqueville's own, not always successful, efforts at definition. Such an exercise would touch, almost automatically, on nearly all of Tocqueville's essential ideas. Instead of definitions, Tocqueville's book could perhaps be read by way of his questions. A careful listing and thoughtful consideration of the major questions or dilemmas that he posed for modern democratic societies would also lead readers to his key themes.

More strictly political approaches to Tocqueville's work could also serve to reveal his essential message. Readers could, for example, simply lay out fully and in detail his political program, his specific recommendations for enhancing the advantages and avoiding the disadvantages of democracy. What ultimately were his remedies and recommendations for the democratic age? What did he mean by a new political science? A closely related way to unlock his *Democracy* is to concentrate on the critics and champions of democracy, cataloguing both the common charges against and the presumed benefits of democracy, and looking closely at what Tocqueville has to say to each side of the debate. How did he attempt to win over the enemies of democracy? What words of caution did he address to the friends of democracy? What kind of coalition of men of good will did he hope to create?

Tocqueville himself put this organizing principle into words:

Principal object. Somewhere. I want to make *everyone* understand that a democratic social state is an invincible necessity in our time. Dividing then my readers into enemies and friends of democracy, I want to make the first understand that for a democratic social state to be tolerable, for it to be able to produce order, progress, in a word, to avoid all the evils that they anticipate, at least the greatest ones, they must at all costs hasten to give *enlightenment* and *liberty* to the people who already have such a social state.

To the second, I want to make them understand that democracy cannot give the happy fruits that they expect from it except by combining it with morality, spiritualism, beliefs. . . . I thus try to unite all honest and generous minds within a small number of common ideas. As for the question of knowing if such a social state is or is not the best that humanity can have, may God himself say so. Only God can say."[55]

The survey of themes we have just completed clearly combines these options for analysis. Without exhaustively or exclusively pursuing any one possible approach, we have tried to learn from each. This turning and returning from multiple perspectives has, I hope, clarified the meaning of Tocqueville's masterpiece.

As we have examined some of Tocqueville's major themes, we have noted a few important differences between the 1835 and 1840 parts of his work, such as the shifting images of democratic despotism and the move away from America. But we also uncovered several instances of comments and conversations from Tocqueville's travel notes carried directly, almost unchanged, into his *Democracy*. And we encountered still other examples of ideas first touched upon in the 1835 text and then expanded and developed in 1840. We have seen that, in many ways, the second portion of Tocqueville's book grew almost organically out of the first.

Our review of Tocqueville's themes also allows us to reflect further on the ways in which he thought and wrote. Perhaps most fundamentally, we have seen that his ideas were never static. Even the text of his *Democracy* is amended in successive revisions, in marginal comments and queries that he inserted into his working manuscript. And in postpublication efforts found in his correspondence, he tried, still again, to explain and restate the essential message of his book. From 1831 (and before) to 1840 (and beyond) he never ceased to raise questions and to reconsider previous conclusions.

Tocqueville relied on certain mental habits or techniques. He used the tool of comparison to help clarify his thinking, especially, as we have noted, by juxtaposing aristocracy and democracy, or America and France. He liked to think in opposing pairs and then struggled to sort out the limits of those pairs. Rejecting any tendency toward a single or absolute principle, he preferred moderation and pluralism. In drafts of his final chapter he declared:

> It is necessary to find in some part of the work, in the foreword or the last chapter, the idea of the *middle* that has been so dishonored in our times. Show that there is a firm, clear, voluntary way to see and to grasp the truth between two extremes. To conceive and to say that the truth is not in an absolute system. Dare to say somewhere . . . that the system of probabilities is the only true one, the only *human* one, provided that probability causes you to act as energetically as certitude. All that is poorly said, but the germ is there."[56]

Open-ended definitions, annoyingly elastic terms, and unanswered questions mark Tocqueville's thinking and writing. As a result, his ideas present both rich nuance and great complexity; readers are left with ambiguities, contradictions (or near contradictions), unresolved dilemmas, and ranges of possible causes and results, of possible difficulties and solutions. Tocqueville always proves hard to pin down.

8

What Else Does Tocqueville Have to Say about America?

WHAT IS SPECIFIC TO AMERICA?

Tocqueville's *DEMOCRACY IN AMERICA* CAN BE UNDER-stood as two interlocking books, one about America, the other about democracy. As we have observed, Tocqueville himself realized the difficulty of separating what was "American" from what was "democratic" and described the 1835 portion of his book as more "American" and 1840 as more "democratic." One of the many ways to read *Democracy in America* is through the lens of the New World experience. Tocqueville's intellectual encounter with America stands as an unavoidable chapter in the story of his book.

Our discussion of the major themes of his work disclosed many of Tocqueville's most important discoveries while in the United States and revealed how those new findings stimulated and, to a degree, changed his thinking. For Tocqueville, the American republic provided additional meanings of equality, democracy, and liberty and helped to deepen his understanding of those fundamental concepts. It illustrated some particular democratic dangers, such as tyranny of the majority; instability in laws, administration, and policy; mediocre political leadership; and public discourse focused on flattery of the people. And it exemplified a mixed system for pursuing major national projects and achieving the proper balance of private and public involvement in economic development. Perhaps most significantly, America also suggested, by way of example, most of the key elements of the political program offered by Tocqueville in his book.

Tocqueville's voyage to the New World taught him several fundamental lessons about how to preserve liberty in the age of democracy.

In America, he witnessed first hand the social, political, economic, and moral advantages of local liberties, decentralization, and the scattering of power; the value of associations for overcoming individual isolation and promoting civic participation and public life; the importance of civil and political rights; the value of the doctrine of interest well understood; and the need to blend the spirit of religion and the spirit of liberty and to foster religion in democratic societies, especially by upholding the separation of church and state. Each of these themes, essential to Tocqueville's suggested remedies for democratic dangers, emerged in large part from what he had experienced during his journey. So America did indeed color his image of democracy.

But some of the observations about the United States found in Tocqueville's working papers and book remain more specific to America than to democracy in general. One of his enduring purposes was to depict the great American republic in grand outline for his readers. Three topics in particular serve as good examples: the North American physiography, the Federal Constitution, and the future of the three races in America. More broadly, we also need to look at the many uses of America for Tocqueville: as a mirror, a model, a countermodel, an example, and an exception. As we have noted, Tocqueville often made much of American singularity.

THE AMERICAN SETTING

See in vol. 1 (1835): part 1, chap. 1; and chap. 8, pp. 149–61; part 2, chap. 9, pp. 265–74; and chap. 10, pp. 348–79 and pp. 384–96.

Reflecting his belief that physical circumstances inescapably influence the course of any nation, Tocqueville began both his portrait and his book with a broad physiographic description.[1] In a few pages, Tocqueville set forth several fundamental features of the American environment. He described the sheer size of the North American continent, its rich resources and vast potential, its distance from the Old World, and its relative emptiness. As noted in his chapter, the area occupied by the United States possessed a mysterious history of previous peoples, unknown even to its then current Native American inhabitants, but Tocqueville presented the continent as essentially set aside by Providence, a land waiting for later discovery and exploitation by civilized man.

For Tocqueville, the Anglo-Americans seemed engaged in what amounted to a second discovery of the New World. He saw as inevitable the relentless expansion westward into the Mississippi Valley (and beyond) and the eventual subjugation of the entire continent, treating that process almost as an additional environmental given. Adopting an elegiac tone in his opening chapter, he saw the spectacle, which meant both the disappearance of the American wilderness and the destruction of the native populations, as at once magnificent and terrible to behold.

According to Tocqueville, the physical circumstances and geographic setting helped to explain why the Anglo-Americans were able to survive as a large federal republic, to manage with almost no visible government, a small army, and a rudimentary bureaucracy, and in general, to enjoy the privilege of making mistakes in some of their laws, policies, and procedures. Consistently, in his travel notes, letters home, working papers, and published text, Tocqueville cited the physiographic situation of the United States as one of the causes that helped to explain its success and prosperity.

THE FEDERAL CONSTITUTION

See in vol. 1 (1835): part 1, chap. 5, esp. p. 56; chap. 6; and chap. 8, esp. pp. 143–61; part 2, chap. 10, pp. 348–79.

Although Tocqueville understood the founding instrument as, in part, a resume of political principles and institutional arrangements that had first appeared in the towns and states of America, he also presented the Constitution as a remarkably original document, created by men of rare wisdom and statesmanship, and he argued that it was superior in many ways to the various state constitutions. The nature of the Union fascinated Tocqueville; in his analysis, he called American federalism "an entirely new theory that will be marked as a great discovery in the political science of our day."[2] In a penetrating analysis, he described the way in which the states and central government, with separate and somewhat defined spheres of responsibility and power, were nonetheless intricately interlocked. Tocqueville also knew that when the separate responsibilities of the states and federal government were unclear, it was the Supreme Court, a federal institution, that had the ultimate right to determine jurisdiction; Tocqueville perceptively recognized this power as perhaps, in the long run, the most serious breach of state sovereignty. He noted as well that, under the United States Constitution, the central government, following a principle unknown in previous federations, addressed individuals not through the member states, but directly.

To describe this innovative constitutional structure, Tocqueville searched once again for a new word. The American Union, he realized, was neither a usual federation or confederation, nor a unitary state. In the working manuscript of the 1835 portion of his book, Tocqueville remarked, "The government of the United States is not truly speaking a *federal* government. It is a national government of which the powers are limited. *Important*. Blend of *national* and *federal* in the Constitution."[3] In his text he conceded: "The new word that ought to express the new thing still does not exist."[4]

Among the institutional principles and arrangements embodied in the federal Constitution, Tocqueville highly praised the role of the judiciary, pointing out the originality of the right of American courts to declare laws unconstitutional and noting how difficult political issues in the United States often ended up before the courts as matters for judges to decide.[5] The independence and activist role of the American judiciary served not only to preserve the balance of powers, but also to check the potential dangers of both legislative despotism and tyranny of the majority. "Judicial power," he declared in one of his drafts for the 1835 portion of his book, "[is] the most original and most difficult part to understand of all the American Constitution. Elsewhere there have been confederations, a representative system, a democracy; but nowhere a judicial power organized as that of the Union."[6]

Tocqueville also approved of bicameralism and the indirect election of the Senate, noting how these measures again lessened the dangers of both legislative despotism and impetuous actions arising from popular passions (possible tyranny of the majority). We need to recall that Tocqueville worried about any unlimited power, including the whole people speaking directly. He specifically condemned both the election of judges and the growing use of mandates in the United States, and even predicted erroneously that the trend in America would be toward greater use of indirect election as a filter for popular impulses.[7] Despite his calls for wider suffrage and broader participation, he remained wary of an unrestrained and unfiltered public voice.

More broadly, as a good student of Montesquieu, he applauded the principle of the separation and balance of powers. In his account, Tocqueville described the American president as the weakest part of the arrangement. But he carefully pointed out to his readers that the prerogatives of the chief executive were immense, and he accurately predicted that, if the United States became repeatedly involved in wars and major foreign affairs, the president would become enormously powerful.[8] In the 1830s, he realized that the prerogatives of the office were more potential than actual. In this, Tocqueville's analysis was correct. But he did miss one of the important developments in the history of the presidency initiated by Andrew Jackson, who, while Tocqueville was in America, was redefining the president as the sole representative not simply of a state or congressional district, but of the entire nation. If Tocqueville had recognized this claim, he would perhaps have been even more assertive about the potential future role of the American chief executive.

THE FUTURE OF THE THREE RACES

See in vol. 1 (1835): part 2, chap. 7, pp. 248–49; and chap. 10.

Tocqueville devoted the longest chapter in the 1835 *Democracy* to other matters more specific to America. This chapter, entitled "Some Considerations on the Present State and the Probable Future of the Three Races That Inhabit the Territory of the United States," was not part of his original plan for the 1835 portion of his book. His remarks about Native Americans and blacks (slave and free) closely parallel the discussions found in Beaumont's *Marie*, which perhaps explains his initial reluctance to include the piece.

Tocqueville began his chapter with two long initial segments in which he dealt with what he foresaw as the inevitable destruction of the native tribes; the consequences, for both black and white Americans, of the institution of slavery; and the brutal treatment by Anglo-Americans of both Native Americans and blacks. He also recounted and usually condemned, sometimes with sarcasm, the various justifications that white Americans habitually advanced for their policies and behavior.[9]

Tocqueville astutely grasped the inverse fates of the red and black minorities. Native Americans met the Anglo-American desire to "civilize" them, to make them like white Americans, with fierce pride, steadfastly rejecting any assimilation. And by either law or custom, blacks both slave and free who wanted to become full and free members of American society found themselves held apart and kept in an inferior status. Tocqueville knew from his own travels that free blacks in America were thoroughly segregated, without basic rights, and were often caught in poverty. In the states of the North, where slavery had been abolished, the prejudice against free blacks was paradoxically even more intense. The problem of racism in the United States, he remarked, would long outlast slavery.

Tocqueville's treatment of slavery remains remarkable. Modern servitude, unlike ancient slavery, he reminded his readers, was based on race. He condemned slavery as immoral and indefensible. He explored the corrosive effects of slavery not only on the slave, but also on the master. And he portrayed the institution as the root cause of the moral and material differences between North and South. According to Tocqueville, slavery shaped southern mores and attitudes and determined the distinctive features of the southern economy. To slavery, he attributed at least indirectly the growing tensions and distrust between the two sections; slavery, he asserted, made the pace of economic growth in the South relatively slow compared to that of the North. "The weak," he wrote in his text, "rarely have confidence in the justice and reason of the strong."[10]

Tocqueville saw no near or easy end to slavery in America, and feared the possibility of a race war in the southern states. He believed, however, that slavery would eventually disappear. "[Whatever] the efforts of

Americans of the South to preserve slavery, they will not succeed at it forever. Slavery contracted to a single point on the globe, attacked by Christianity as unjust, by political economy as fatal; slavery, in the midst of the democratic freedom and enlightenment of our age, is not an institution that can endure. It will cease by the deed of the slave or the master. In both cases, one must expect great misfortunes."[11] Here was one of the few places in his *Democracy* where Tocqueville expressed profound pessimism about the American future.

In one sense, Tocqueville's long chapter on the three races in America is an extended treatment of two of the most glaring inequalities in a society otherwise marked by a surprisingly thorough equality. Both Native Americans and blacks were excluded from the democratic equality enjoyed by the Anglo-American inhabitants of the United States. The opening parts of the chapter also deal, of course, with American racism.[12] The white American majority assumed an aristocracy of skin color and exercised a kind of tyranny based on race. Both Tocqueville and Beaumont, who each rejected all racist theories, realized that the fundamental issue in the United States did not involve slavery, despite its horrors, but an underlying racism that would not disappear with the end of slavery and might even worsen.

When Tocqueville shifted his attention to the current situation and probable future of the Anglo-Americans, he addressed the future of both the Union and republican institutions in America; the current political issues facing Jacksonian America;[13] the prosperity and economic development of the United States, which Tocqueville called almost revolutionary in speed; the coming greatness of American commerce, with Tocqueville erroneously predicting a commercial rather than an industrial future for the United States; and the American drive to occupy and dominate the entire continent, with yet another prediction, this time accurate, of events in Texas and conflict with Mexico.

Although arguments in his drafts were sometimes more negative, the published text of Tocqueville's 1835 *Democracy* presented, on the whole, a more positive assessment of the future of the Union.[14] Shared material interests and a common American ideology, Tocqueville contended, would probably hold the Union together, despite sectional differences and tensions. In the long run, however, he doubted the likelihood of the continued existence of a vast and densely populated federal republic. He also argued that for over forty years the federal government had been growing weaker in the face of state assertions of power.[15] By 1838, in drafts for the foreword to the 1840 *Democracy*, Tocqueville realized his mistake and wrote: "Admit my error. The weakening of the federal bond."[16] Unfortunately, however, this recognition would never appear in his published text.

AMERICAN EXCEPTIONALISM

Throughout the pages of both portions of his book, Tocqueville treated America's physical and historical circumstances as unique. The United States, he observed, enjoyed not only extraordinary physiographic assets, but also highly unusual historical advantages; he described American society as unencumbered by the legacy of feudalism or the experience of revolution. And, as we have just seen, he presented much of the American federal structure and the situation of the Native Americans, blacks, and Anglo-Americans as specific to America. So his chapters on physiography, history, and the three races lead us into one of the persistent dilemmas of Tocqueville's *Democracy*: the issue of American exceptionalism.

The message of American exceptionalism appeared elsewhere in Tocqueville's book. We have already noted how, according to Tocqueville, Anglo-Americans, because of their free institutions and particular mores, remained relatively exempt from the threats of individualism and the new democratic despotism, and, because of their good morals, regular habits, and religious beliefs, largely immune from the worst effects of materialism. Less positively, Tocqueville treated the United States as an exception culturally. Both parts of his *Democracy* portray American society as suffering from literary and intellectual mediocrity; but for Tocqueville, as we have noted, that weakness did not exemplify any necessary connection between democracy and culture.

If the American situation was unique, however, what lessons could America possibly provide to other nations less happily situated? How could the democratic experience of an exceptional America be applied to other societies and, more pointedly, to France? To escape this dilemma, Tocqueville once again sought the middle ground. In his book, he carefully pointed out how the United States was different, but he also insisted that America provided useful lessons to other nations about how best to enhance democratic benefits and avoid democratic pitfalls.

At times, when America could directly teach France and other nations, Tocqueville cited American society simply as a democratic example to follow, at least in broad outline. At other times, he depicted the United States as an exception, but gave as reasons for the American exemption the very solutions that he wanted his readers to consider, free institutions and the habits of liberty, for example. And sometimes, where American lessons and experience did not apply, he treated the New World republic as purely an exception. This shifting use of the principle of exceptionalism allowed Tocqueville to fit America, as he desired, into the particular issue before him and his readers. Like the concepts of equality and democracy, the notion of exceptionalism remained complex and elastic enough in Tocqueville's thinking to take on the coloring that best suited his argument at a given moment.

OTHER FUNCTIONS OF AMERICA

America, which served as one of Tocqueville's essential sources, as a point of comparison and contrast, and as a (sometimes) unique counterpoint, played several other roles in Tocqueville's *Democracy*. The American republic functioned as a mirror to show French and other readers how their own emerging democratic societies would soon look and what advantages and disadvantages they should expect (America as a way to see the future); as a model to suggest how best to cope with advancing democracy and, more specifically, to demonstrate the laws and mores that constituted Tocqueville's political program (America as the well-ordered and healthy democracy); as a countermodel to illustrate certain potential democratic risks (America as a cautionary tale); and finally, as a foreign society of great interest to those who simply wanted to learn more about the New World republic (America as a destination for armchair travelers). These functions are closely intertwined and not easily distinguished, but perhaps the common thread for all was America as a source of lessons for Tocqueville and his readers.

Tocqueville presented, in his introduction and elsewhere, an idealized America, the example of a stable and well-regulated democracy. As a model, the United States subsumed, in the broadest sense, all of the lessons that Tocqueville drew from his journey. But more specifically, America transformed Tocqueville's concept of a republic.

The Americans, Tocqueville quickly learned during his visit, had an idea of a republic very different from the image common in France. In June 1831, he wrote to Louis de Kergorlay about a seemingly universal opinion among Americans.

> I have not yet been able to overhear, in a conversation with anyone, no matter to what rank in society they belong, the idea that a republic is not the best possible government. . . . The great majority understands republican principles in the most democratic sense. . . . But that a republic is a good government, that it is natural for human societies, no one seems to doubt— priests, magistrates, businessmen, artisans. That is an opinion that is so general and so little discussed . . . , that one could almost call it a belief.[17]

In the 1835 *Democracy*, Tocqueville made this discovery explicit. "What one understands by republic in the United States," he declared,

> is the slow and tranquil action of society on itself. It is a regular state really founded on the enlightened will of the people. It is a conciliating government, in which resolutions ripen for a long time, are discussed slowly and executed only when mature. Republicans in the United States prize mores, respect beliefs, recognize rights. They profess the opinion that a people ought to be moral, religious and moderate to the degree it is free. What one calls a republic in the United States is the tranquil reign of the majority. The majority, after it has had the time to recognize itself and to certify its existence, is the common source of powers. But the majority itself is not all-powerful. Above it in the moral world are humanity, justice and reason; in the political world, acquired rights. The majority recognizes these two barriers. . . . The ideas of a republic that the Americans have made

for themselves singularly facilitate their use of it and assure its longevity. Among them, if the practice of republican government is often bad, at least the theory is good.[18]

For Tocqueville this idealized image of the tranquil, enlightened, and moderate American republic not only became the symbol of what a well-ordered democracy might be, but also served as a source of hope. The American example, at its best, demonstrated to him that democracy could indeed be regulated or balanced so that democratic societies could be healthy, prosperous, and free; and he, in turn, tried to use the model of the American republic to persuade his readers that such a desirable outcome was possible for democratic nations.

In Tocqueville's *Democracy*, America also sometimes served as a countermodel or as a warning about democratic dangers and threats to liberty. Tyranny of the majority provided the first example. A second, perhaps equally important, was slavery. Tocqueville, seeing the effects of slavery on both slaves and masters, remarked that America probably proved the benefits of equality better by the barbarity and immorality of slavery than by the political freedoms enjoyed by Anglo-Americans.[19] More broadly, he realized that the American republic also risked excessive democracy, especially in the newer states of the West and Southwest. In addition to the dangers of tyranny of the majority, legislative despotism, and the implementation or institutionalization of racism by the Anglo-American majority, he worried about such measures as mandates, which explicitly directed representatives to vote as the constituency required; the direct election of judges, which threatened to turn the judiciary into a mere reflection of popular passions; the assumption that the majority could ignore laws that contradicted its desires and prejudices; and the tendency toward violence and mob rule as an expression of majority will, especially in the localities.

We need always to remember that what Tocqueville said about the American republic is largely in response to his French audience. He had both positive and negative views of America, but in his *Democracy*, he chose to highlight the positive; he wanted to counter French fears and blunt the usual criticisms of democracy. Ultimately, he decided to stress what America got right, rather than dwell on the flaws and failings of the

American republic. An attentive reader will detect his criticisms of the United States; but overall what Tocqueville emphasized in his book were the lessons that America provided to other nations trying to make the best of democracy.

TOCQUEVILLE AND THE AMERICAN EXAMPLE

Our discussion of themes specific to America has uncovered a number of Tocqueville's errors. To some extent, each generation of readers has had a different response to the question of what Tocqueville got wrong; parts of Tocqueville's portrait that have been criticized or rejected at one time have often elicited the opposite judgment at another time, among another set of readers. The same changing perspective remains true even about some of his most notable and honored predictions. Perhaps the best example is his concluding remark in the 1835 *Democracy* that the United States and Russia, as the two emerging empires, would dominate and divide the world, one symbolizing liberty, the other, tyranny.[20] What seemed to readers so prescient a half century ago, now seems a bit outdated.

But, in addition to the mistakes and oversights we have already noticed, we should mention Tocqueville's failure to grasp the emergence, during the Jacksonian era, of radical democracy and such political groups as the workingmen's parties, which were once again based on clear principles or philosophies; his relative silence, except for tangential remarks concerning the revolutionary spirit, about the question of political fanaticism or extremism in democracies; his strange assertion that the wealthy played no part in American politics and his exaggeration of the intergenerational rise and fall of the rich and privileged in American life; and finally, his relative lack of attention to the dangers of the tyranny of minorities. Perhaps each reader should compile a personal list of such errors, omissions, or blind spots. In any case, such an endeavor would not detract from all that Tocqueville got right about America.

In our long examination of the major themes of Tocqueville's book, America appeared not simply as proof or evidence for concepts that predated Tocqueville's voyage to the United States. As we have observed, the American republic also helped to deflect his ideas and reshape or refocus his argument. His New World journey sometimes provided new insights and fresh lessons and took Tocqueville's thinking in unanticipated directions. By presenting the unexpected, the American journey became an essential part of the making of Tocqueville's book.

In addition, the issue of American exceptionalism and the multiple functions of America in Tocqueville's work serve to remind us of the difficulty of judging how the American republic fits into his argument at any given point in his book. Readers need always to be cautious about applying Tocqueville's larger message about democracy, its advantages and disadvantages, its dangers and remedies, to the United States, or moving from America to the broader arena of other democratic societies.

Finally, our thematic review demonstrates yet another important feature of the American example for Tocqueville. Quite arguably, as various commentators have suggested, Tocqueville arrived in the New World already sensitive to most of the worst democratic dangers, including centralization, individual weakness in the face of broad social power, excessive materialism, and many of the shapes of democratic despotism. He also came with a catalogue in mind of other presumed consequences of advancing democracy, most notably chronic social and political instability, even anarchy; disregard for the rule of law; moral and spiritual decay; and the decline of civilization, especially the collapse of high culture.

For this latter list the American republic provided Tocqueville with examples of reassurance that he offered to his readers; in his *Democracy*, he was able to argue, with evidence drawn from America, that these harmful results, though widely feared, were not necessary consequences of democracy. Some supposed democratic dangers, he discovered in the New World, could be discounted, at least partially. But America provided no refutation to the reality of the most important democratic threats to liberty: materialism, individualism, consolidated power, and possible new democratic despotisms. Those dangers could not be denied. Instead, Tocqueville's American journey suggested a variety of effective remedies for democratic ills; much of the political program presented by Tocqueville in both portions of his book emerged in his thinking because of his American experience. The United States, it may be asserted, taught Tocqueville more about democratic solutions than about democratic dangers. Here perhaps was the real lesson of the voyage to America.

PART III

AMERICAN
READINGS OF
TOCQUEVILLE'S
DEMOCRACY

9

How Has Tocqueville's *Democracy* Been Read in America?

AMERICANS HAVE ALWAYS BEEN DRAWN TO TOCQUEVILLE'S *Democracy*. Since the 1830s, the book seems to speak to each successive generation. American readers, past and present, discover Tocqueville wrestling with "current" issues and "contemporary" dilemmas and offering useful insights and advice about their immediate concerns. Somehow, Tocqueville's great work, written over 175 years ago, remains timely and pertinent.

To a degree, however, each generation finds quite different messages in the pages of *Democracy in America*. Almost all readers acknowledge that, while Tocqueville made serious mistakes or missed some things, he got many things amazingly right about America. Yet, from decade to decade, Americans have compiled quite different lists of his successes and failures. So the lessons drawn from Tocqueville's book sometimes differ markedly over time, depending, in part, on changes in American society and culture, and in part on the political persuasion of the reader.

Here we don't need to trace in detail the changing American reception of Tocqueville's work; many informative articles and essays ably review the successive American responses to Tocqueville's *Democracy*. We can, however, briefly note several fundamental features of the story. Initially, Tocqueville's book received a largely positive reaction in the United States. Americans found it refreshing to encounter a mostly favorable presentation of their laws, political institutions, and culture rather than the highly critical or condescending descriptions written by many other contemporary European travelers. During the late nineteenth and early twentieth centuries new editions of Tocqueville's work kept appearing in the United States, and the book continued to be read and studied. Commentators still appreciated the enduring quality of Tocqueville's analysis, but they also often argued that much of his portrait had become somewhat dated. Industrialization, urbanization, immigration, and the new position of the United States in the world had transformed the American republic.

Starting in the 1930s, and especially in the 1940s and 1950s, American readers increasingly began to recognize Tocqueville's *Democracy* not only as a study of American society, but also as an analysis of modern democratic society in general. Tocqueville, they realized, was perhaps not primarily a commentator on America, but a theorist of democracy. This growing appreciation of the broader scope of Tocqueville's work paralleled a general shift in interest from the 1835 to the 1840 half of his *Democracy*. In the nineteenth century editors and commentators usually said little about the second part of Tocqueville's book (1840); they focused almost exclusively on the first part (1835). In sharp contrast, their successors since the mid-twentieth century have increasingly given their attention overwhelmingly to the 1840 portion.

During the last half century, the reputation of Tocqueville's work has not ceased to grow. Why does the book remain so widely read and cited, so admired and influential? Why does it continue over the decades to captivate American readers? As we have seen, Tocqueville's *Democracy* is a remarkably subtle and complex book, with a wide variety of purposes and messages. Like other great reflective works, it speaks to many issues, raises enduring questions, and offers profound insights. Each cohort of Americans is, therefore, able to find in Tocqueville's pages a discussion of the particular issues it faces. In *Democracy in America*, each generation is able to see itself and ponder its own dilemmas.

Tocqueville's book continues to be read (and misread), used (and misused) by readers of widely divergent political perspectives and purposes. To all of them, Tocqueville's work provides valuable, but often quite contradictory, ideas and solutions. His message is sufficiently expansive and complex to appeal to readers across the American political spectrum. With the risk of falling into caricature, we need to examine, in summary, a few of the current readings of Tocqueville's *Democracy*.

CONSERVATIVE READINGS

During the last thirty years Tocqueville has become the darling of the right. For several decades, readers with a conservative perspective have dominated the American interpretation of his *Democracy*. Conservatives find several fundamental themes in Tocqueville's book especially appealing. First, they discover in Tocqueville confirmation that the great democratic danger is administrative centralization, the new soft despotism of the welfare state. We have already discussed the various ways in which Tocqueville's warnings about centralization have been received in contemporary America. To readers on the right, Tocqueville's book wonderfully supports their condemnation of the relentlessly increasing scope and intrusion of government, especially of the federal government, in the United States since the early twentieth century.

Second, many contemporary conservatives applaud Tocqueville's description of advancing democracy as a global phenomenon and his presentation of America as the universal model of democracy. From these premises, it follows for some that the United States has a unique mission in the world. As a great nation, America is called upon to spread democracy forcefully and to carry its own values and perspectives into the rest of the world. Some on the right especially notice and appreciate Tocqueville's desire for great nations that pursue larger universal goals; they favor modern campaigns for democracy that parallel the civilizing mission of France celebrated by Tocqueville in the nineteenth century.

Third, some conservatives find in Tocqueville's pages warnings that echo (or foreshadow) their deepest moral and spiritual concerns. We have seen that Tocqueville worried about what he called the softening of the human soul during democratic times. At its worst, democracy, he observed, could mean a disastrous leveling; the stifling of the exceptional; the rejection of any cultural, intellectual, or moral excellence; and a refusal to follow or even to recognize any elite, no matter how meritorious. From this perspective, human greatness, in the democratic age, finds itself at risk. Many readers on the right agree deeply with these fears. Their lament is for nothing less than the loss of the ideal of the noble society. For them, Tocqueville seems brilliantly to anticipate their own

critique of modern Western society since the Enlightenment as following a downward spiral toward mediocrity and spiritual and moral decay.
With this judgment in mind, such readers interpret Tocqueville as a grim
prophet, stressing not the more positive features of the modern world
that he presented as a partisan of democracy, but the negative implications of advancing equality that Tocqueville also set forth, so carefully
and persuasively, in his book.

Moral concerns also lead readers on the right to highlight Tocqueville's
presentation of religion as essential for the health of any democratic society. His belief that democracy without faith leads to despotism and his
call to "spiritualize" democratic societies are both strongly commended.
Especially in this age of resurgent religion in the United States, Tocqueville's astute treatment of religion as a foundational element in American
society remains a favored theme among conservatives.

Finally, still another current of conservative understanding of Tocqueville demands our attention. No true society, he insisted in his book, could
exist without shared values or common mores. When some conservative
commentators apply this requirement to today's America, they argue
that during the last half century interest groups in the United States have
developed an exaggerated sense of their own identity and entitlement;
such groups, they assert, uphold and defend only their own special rights,
without sufficient concern for the needs of the larger community. Reflecting their understanding of Tocqueville, these interpreters worry that
America has become a collection of self-serving blocs without a common identity, an essentially fragmented society no longer held together
by the shared mores that Tocqueville so admired. For them, the America
so praised by Tocqueville is disappearing.

LIBERAL READINGS

As just noted, dominant interpretations of Tocqueville's *Democracy* for
the past few decades have come largely from the right. So pervasive a
trend has caused some liberal or progressive readers to accept conservative readings and, in reaction, to reject Tocqueville's work as a fundamentally misleading portrait of America and an inadequate guide to

modern democratic society. For other interpreters on the left, however, Tocqueville's book continues to provide useful ideas that support their own opinions and judgments. What are some of the liberal readings of Tocqueville's *Democracy*?

First, many liberals commend Tocqueville's condemnation of unrestrained capitalism as the potential source of terrible new inequalities and as a profound moral danger to the working classes, who are brutalized, as well as to the industrial classes, who are rendered indifferent. Tocqueville, as they read him, emphatically does not see democratic freedom and unregulated free enterprise as inseparable twins.

Second, some readers on the left notice that, according to Tocqueville, a healthy and free democracy requires a rough material equality. They find this argument attractive, and understand Tocqueville as saying that extreme inequality not only undermines human potential, but also destroys any genuine liberty. For them, Tocqueville, in his book, asserts the need for a measure of distributive justice. He insists, they remind us, that democracy is more just than aristocracy precisely because it brings about a more equitable sharing of the good things of the earth. If some conservatives focus on what Tocqueville said about the *noble* society, some liberals, in response, stress what he said about the *just* society.

Here, moral concerns from a liberal perspective parallel the moral critique of democracy familiar in conservative interpretations. Tocqueville the moralist is welcomed by the left as well as by the right. For liberals, the rough distributive justice required by democracy permits all human beings, not just certain castes or classes, to develop fully in mind, body, and spirit. Liberal commentators also note and commend Tocqueville's other moral premise. For him, as they read his book, participating fully in a shared public life, holding and exercising full rights as a citizen of the larger community, expands the human soul; democracy as participation has an essential moral function.

Third, many progressives find support in Tocqueville's pages for their belief in the central importance of civil and political rights; they welcome his eloquent insistence that liberty, in the abstract, needs to be embodied in specific rights, for even the least and most vulnerable citizen, and that those liberties must be meticulously and faithfully honored and upheld. For them, Tocqueville's *Democracy* contains powerful "rights talk."

Fourth, readers on the left appreciate Tocqueville's argument that one of the most essential definitions of democracy is wide participation in public life. For them, Tocqueville seems to endorse efforts not only to extend civil and political rights as widely as possible, but also to engage in vigorous grassroots and community organizing. As they read his work, democracy, without broad citizen empowerment, is a sham.

Finally, as many liberals understand Tocqueville, his book warns about oppression not only from government or public institutions, but also from private concentrations of power, including corporations and their owners, and from groups of citizens who attempt by violence or by public pressure to bend dissenting individuals or minorities to their views and behavior. Many on the left also approve Tocqueville's observation that tyranny in the United States was likely to come not from the federal government, but from the states, to be exercised in the localities. And they endorse his vision of the role of government, which he wanted to be neither weak nor indolent.

LIBERTARIAN READINGS

Libertarian readings of Tocqueville's *Democracy* merge with certain stripes of both conservative and liberal interpretation. What, in particular, appeals to libertarians in Tocqueville's work? First, they salute Tocqueville's conviction that liberty is the greatest good and should always be the central concern, especially in times of democracy (his "holy cult of liberty"). Second, they agree with Tocqueville that democracy, by dissolving traditional supports and by breeding a sense of isolation and powerlessness, puts the individual at risk. For libertarians, individual independence is gravely threatened in modern society, especially by public or governmental institutions and by the dictates of public or mass opinion. A corollary closely follows: the best government or public authority is the least. As we have noted, this principle is not exactly what Tocqueville argued. His work does, however, strongly reject any consolidated power that threatens the individual, and Tocqueville wrote eloquently about the jealous protection of individual liberty. On these matters, libertarians read his book with particular satisfaction.

COMMUNITARIAN READINGS

Communitarians come from various places in the political spectrum, and like libertarians, often reflect conservative or liberal perspectives; they elude easy labels of right and left. But communitarian interpreters find particular intellectual support in Tocqueville's alerts about democratic individualism. Perhaps their central concern is the decline of American social capital. They lament excessive privatism; the diminishing level of participation in associations, in localities, and in other arenas of society and government; the collapse of a shared public life; the rise of gated communities; and the decay of traditional American mores (habits of the heart). For communitarian readers, the great democratic danger—pointed out by Tocqueville—is the loss of civic spirit. They also praise his emphasis on associations and local involvements as instruments for encouraging healthy habits of citizenship and his description of religion as a force for reaffirming shared values and for diverting people from narrow, materialistic interests toward higher commitments. For communitarians, Tocqueville's *Democracy* provides a road map to true citizenship and community. They echo both the progressive focus on broad grassroots participation and the conservative emphasis on religion and small government.

ALL OF THESE INTERPRETATIONS—FROM RIGHT OR LEFT, from libertarian or communitarian—are legitimately grounded in elements of Tocqueville's argument; each is able to find support in the pages of his book. As we have seen, in notes to himself and in letters to his friends, Tocqueville repeatedly attempted to summarize his argument and to capture an essential message that, despite his efforts, remained somewhat elusive. As a result, readers of diverse viewpoints and political persuasions have found in his work lessons pertinent to their own times and useful for their own understanding and purposes. Tocqueville's words have always spoken to his readers in multiple and sometimes in somewhat unintended ways.

Tocqueville was aware of this phenomenon very early. Just after the appearance of the 1835 segment of his *Democracy*, he remarked, "I please many people of conflicting opinions, not because they understand me, but because they find in my work, by considering it only from a single side, arguments favorable to their passion of the moment."[1] And as he drafted the 1840 portion, he added: "[It] delights me to see the different features that are given to me according to the political passions of the person who cites me. . . . They absolutely want to make me a party man and I am not that in the least; they assign to me passions and I have only opinions, or rather I have only one passion, the love of liberty and human dignity."[2]

So all readers need to remain vigilant about what they presume to find in the pages of Tocqueville's *Democracy*. Understanding Tocqueville's book is never straightforward. Tocqueville's striking ability to appeal to readers across a wide spectrum of opinion and outlook is one reason for the enduring attraction of his work.

Do the various readings we have reviewed have anything in common? Strikingly, contemporary American interpretations of Tocqueville's book have abandoned the early impulse of Americans to focus on Tocqueville's praise for their laws, institutions, and habits. As late as the 1950s, many American readers emphasized Tocqueville's favorable portrayal of the free American republic and placed that positive assessment against the horrors of the twentieth-century totalitarian regimes of right and left. Today's readings almost always concentrate, instead, on the major democratic dangers catalogued by Tocqueville. As we have observed, he often specifically exempted the United States—for a variety of reasons—from such threats as democratic individualism, administrative centralization, and excessive materialism. But current American understandings do not make the same assumption. They essentially reject his reassurances about American exceptionalism. His *Democracy* is now read less for what he praised about the United States than for what he warned democratic society against. Today Tocqueville's portrait of America is seen through a much darker lens.

Perhaps the phenomenon of widely divergent interpretations best serves to remind us that no single, "correct" reading of Tocqueville's *De-*

mocracy exists. Even when readers conscientiously keep Tocqueville's fundamental convictions and purposes in mind and understand the principal features of his approach and mental habits, they nonetheless find very different messages in his book. According to Tocqueville, for example, an inescapable tension exists in the modern world between liberty and equality. (This is one of his basic convictions.) For some readers, this opposition reinforces their suspicion of equality as a threat to liberty and their dread that, in the end, excessive equality will undermine freedom and the possibility of human greatness. For others, the same tension fits their conviction that without basic equality, liberty is hollow; they fear that extreme calls for liberty can become an excuse for a corrosive inequality that will, as well, ultimately undercut the best possibilities of humanity. Tocqueville's insight about liberty and equality in democratic societies remains the starting point. But where finally does he place the appropriate limits of this particular pair? In the pull between conflicting interpretations of his argument, Tocqueville remains difficult to capture.

CONCLUDING REFLECTIONS

WHY HAS *DEMOCRACY IN AMERICA* LASTED SO WELL? After our review of the contexts, themes, and readings of Tocqueville's book, we can suggest several reasons. Tocqueville's mental habits of searching for the limits of opposing pairs, of avoiding fixed and absolute positions, of seeking moderate grounds, of constantly revisiting ideas, and of using elastic terms and concepts make his work highly nuanced and complex. In addition, his conclusions almost always remain tentative and uncertain. Instead of a single, final answer, he offers his readers plural and contingent solutions. In his *Democracy*, Tocqueville presents a political program, broadly understood, which proposes remedies for democratic ills. But no single, definitive *Tocquevillian* platform or vision exists to rally disciples. Instead, the true strength of his book, it can be argued, rests not with his conclusions, but with the questions he raises and the dilemmas he explores with his readers. The sweep of his approach also enriches and enlivens his work. For Tocqueville, all areas of human society were linked; changes in one area inevitably caused modifications in the others. In his *Democracy*, Tocqueville tried to discover and understand those interconnections, and then to describe them to his readers.

So Tocqueville's authorial preference for complexity and ambiguity, for probabilities and approximations; his quest for explanations, his unshakable impulse to pose questions and challenge assumptions; and the sheer scope of his enterprise, all help to explain the continuing fascination of his *Democracy*. These very characteristics also occasionally lead to contradictory, or seemingly contradictory, opinions; to the use of chameleon words that shifted according to Tocqueville's purposes and allowed him to escape moments of decision; and to meanings that were sometimes vague and difficult to grasp.

Tocqueville wrote his book with many purposes in mind; his varied goals serve as yet another complication. Throughout this volume we have compiled a considerable list of the key purposes of *Democracy*. In his book he wanted to demonstrate how to make France free, prosperous, and stable; how to preserve liberty in the face of equality; and how to uphold individual independence in the age of democracy. He also wanted to identify the democratic dangers and despotisms most to be feared. In addition, we have watched Tocqueville offering an analysis of American society, politics, and culture; presenting a running contrast of aristocratic and democratic societies; exposing the advantages and disadvantages of democracy and suggesting proposals to maximize the first and minimize the second; and giving an extended response, a long exercise in reassurance, to counter many of the most common criticisms of democracy in his time.

In our study of *Democracy in America*, we have also encountered and need to recognize another special key for helping to understand Tocqueville's book. Tocqueville's travel diaries, letters home, initial plans, successive drafts, marginal notes, and other working papers often help in significant ways to supplement and explain his published text. Paradoxically, to understand better what appears in Tocqueville's book, readers need to be aware of what does *not* appear in its pages. We have already described the variety of contexts in which Tocqueville thought and wrote and the importance of those settings for comprehending the argument of his *Democracy*. What is absent serves as yet another context necessary for readers to know. The full story of the making of his book becomes essential for grasping its message.

One central theme of Tocqueville's work is the irresistible march of democracy. In the early twenty-first century, who can doubt this message? Democracy, as defined by Tocqueville, implied wide participation in public life, broad civic communication and interaction, and a refusal to allow any entrenched authority to stand permanently apart in some separate and markedly unequal privileged status. Despite familiar complaints about the collapse of traditional forms of community and civic involvement, today's technology, it can be persuasively argued, has brought about a different sort of connection that has proved to be an extremely potent form of democratic energy. Tocqueville's democratic revolution continues to unfold before our eyes.

Or does it? Given the starts and stops, the advances and retreats of democracy and the recurring rise of horrendous despotisms, especially during the past one hundred years, perhaps we should reconsider Tocqueville's assumption and ours. Was Tocqueville wrong about the inevitability of democracy? The issue is too important for us to treat as a closed question.

Our summary of readings, presented above, included by choice only American views. Before ending, we need to acknowledge the long and vigorous traditions of interpreting Tocqueville's book in France, England, and other Western nations. Moreover, during the past few decades, the appreciation and application of Tocqueville's *Democracy* has spread not only to Eastern Europe, but also to many other countries around the world. Especially in Japan and China, there is now intense interest in Tocqueville's work. This ability to attract readers from widely divergent societies and cultures again testifies to the lasting appeal of his book. Fascination with *Democracy in America* has become worldwide, and has produced fresh global perspectives on the meaning of Tocqueville's message.

Finally, we need to remember the moral dimension of *Democracy in America*. We have met Tocqueville in many guises, including historian, political theorist, philosopher, sociologist, psychologist, social psychologist, and political economist. But many passages in his book reveal Tocqueville as a moralist and underscore his concerns about the moral consequences of democracy. His arguments for public participation and for communication and intellectual exchange among human beings, for example, assume a necessary connection between the moral and political worlds, and focus ultimately on ways to nurture the human spirit and enhance human dignity. For Tocqueville the moralist, achieving full human potential was impossible without the liberty of each person to engage in the social and political community. Here perhaps was the essence of what he hoped to preserve and promote in the age of democracy.

PART IV

TOOLS FOR USE

GLOSSARY

WHAT ARE SOME OF THE KEY TERMS
IN TOCQUEVILLE'S *DEMOCRACY*?

THIS GLOSSARY PRESENTS A LIST OF KEY TERMS USED IN Tocqueville's *Democracy*. Readers need to remember, however, that Tocqueville introduces and discusses his major concepts not only in particular chapters or sections, but also in scattered passages throughout his book. One of the pleasures of reading his *Democracy* is encountering additional references and reflections about fundamental ideas in unexpected places. So the page citations that follow are far from exhaustive; they are intended only to point readers to Tocqueville's introductory remarks or extensive discussions about a term. The glossary included here also refers readers to pages or sections of this companion where a term is defined and discussed. In each case, the page number where a definition is found is given in **bold, italicized** type. Definitions are not repeated here.

	Companion (chapter: page)	*Democracy* (UCP) (page)
Aristocracy	2: 35–36 3: *50* 4: 63	*Throughout, but see esp.* intro., 8, 170–72, 234–35, 530–32
Associations (and spirit of association)	4: 65–68 6: 105–8, esp. *105*, 116–17	166–72, 172–80, 180–86, 489–92, 493–95, 496–500, 667–68
Centralization	2: 19, 35–36 5: 83–100, esp. *84–86* 6: 116–17 7: 122–26, 137–39	52–53, 53–55, 82–93, 143– 46, 165, 646–50, 661–65
Circumstances	3: *51–52*, 54–55 8: 147–48	19–27, 149–61, 264–74, 292–95, 348–79, 384–96

	Companion (chapter: page)	*Democracy* (UCP) (page)
Materialism	3: 52–55 5: 72–77	265–74, 384–90, 469–72, 506–09, 511–14, 514–17, 519–520
Mores	3: *51*, 51–52, 54–55 4: 65–68, 71 6: 101–3, 112–14 7: 139–42	264–65, 274–75, 288–92, 292–98, 358–59 (on American mores), 506–09, 535–41, 558–63, 563–65, 565–67, 567–73, 573–78, 589–99
Point of departure	2: 28 3: *51–52*	27–32, 35–36, 39–44
Race (and races)	2: 43–44 3: 52–55 5: 92 7: 139–40 8: 150–53	23–27, 248–49, 302–96 (esp. 302–48), 469–72, 675–76
Religion (and spirit of religion)	2: 42 3: 54 4: 65 6: 112–14 7: 129	Intro., 10–12, 43–44, 275–88, 403–07, 417–24, 424–26, 504–06, 510–11, 517–21, 522–24, 673–76
Republic (and republicanism)	2: 39 8: 154–57	379–84
Revolutionary spirit (and spirit of revolution)	1: 9–10 4: 64 5: 82 7: 136–37, esp. *137*	Intro., 3–6, 187, 484–85, 587–88, 606–17
Self-interest well understood	6: *108–11*	225–27, 500–03, 504–06, 514–17
Social state	4: *57–58*, 56–64	45–53
Sovereignty of the people	2: 42–43 5: *83*	53–55, 165
Three causes (*see* Circumstances; Laws; Mores)	—	—
Tyranny of the majority	5: 88–92	235–49, 250–64, 298–302, 407–10

GUIDE TO KEY CHAPTERS
AND PASSAGES

WHICH PARTS OF TOCQUEVILLE'S *DEMOCRACY* ARE THE MOST FAMOUS AND ESSENTIAL?

THE FOLLOWING LIST IS MEANT TO INDICATE WHICH chapters, sections, and passages are most essential to notice when reading *Democracy in America*. Every serious reader of Tocqueville's book will, of course, have personal and different interests, purposes, and perspectives and will therefore assemble a somewhat distinctive compilation of key segments, so no single guide can claim to be definitive. The choices presented here are made to highlight Tocqueville's major themes as presented in this volume. In each case, appropriate cross-references to the *Companion* are given to allow easier exploration by the reader.

VOLUME 1 (1835)

Introduction, pp. 3–15
> —*Companion*, chap. 1, pp. 11–12; chap. 3, pp. 49–51; chap. 4, pp. 56–57, 62–63; chap. 6, pp. 115–17; chap. 7, p. 137; chap. 8, pp. 154–56

PART 1

Chap. 2, On the Point of Departure, pp. 27–32, 39–44
> —*Companion*, chap. 2, p. 28; chap. 3, pp. 51–52; chap. 4, pp. 62–65

Chap. 3, Social State of the Anglo-Americans, pp. 45–53
> —*Companion*, chap. 4, pp. 56–64

Chap. 4, On the Principle of Sovereignty of the People, pp. 53–55
> —*Companion*, chap. 4, pp. 58 and 60; chap. 5, p. 83

Chap. 5, p. 56 and On the Township System in America, pp. 57–58; On Township Existence, pp. 61–63; On the Spirit of the Township in New England, pp. 63–65; On the Political Effects of Administrative Decentralization in the United States, pp. 82–93
> —*Companion*, chap. 2, pp. 42–43; chap. 4, pp. 65–68; chap. 5, pp. 84–86, 91–92; chap. 6, pp. 101–5, 115–17; chap. 8, pp. 146–47

SUGGESTIONS FOR
FURTHER READING

The following suggestions are meant to provide a very brief, bare-bones list of books available in English that will be useful for students and others who are reading Tocqueville's *Democracy in America* for the first time. No articles or works in other languages are included. More extensive bibliographies will be found in most of the books cited.

Boesche, Roger, ed. *Alexis de Tocqueville: Selected Letters on Politics and Society.* Translated by James Toupin and Roger Boesche. Berkeley: University of California Press, 1985.

Brogan, Hugh. *Alexis de Tocqueville: A Life.* New Haven: Yale University Press, 2007.

Craiutu, Aurelian, and Sheldon Gellar, eds. *Conversations with Tocqueville: The Global Democratic Revolution in the Twenty-First Century.* Lanham, MD: Lexington Books, 2009.

Craiutu, Aurelian, and Jeremy Jennings, eds. *Tocqueville on America after 1840.* Cambridge: Cambridge University Press, 2009.

Damrosch, Leo. *Tocqueville's Discovery of America.* New York: Farrar, Straus and Giroux, 2010.

Drescher, Seymour, ed. *Tocqueville and Beaumont on Social Reform.* New York: Harper and Row, 1968.

———. *Tocqueville and England.* Cambridge: Harvard University Press, 1964.

Jardin, André. *Tocqueville: A Biography.* Translated by Lydia Davis. New York: Farrar, Straus and Giroux, 1988. (First published in French as *Alexis de Tocqueville (1805–1859)* [Paris: Hachette, 1984].)

Kahan, Alan S. *Alexis de Tocqueville.* New York: Continuum, 2010.

Mancini, Matthew. *Alexis de Tocqueville and American Intellectuals: From His Time to Ours.* Lanham, MD: Rowman and Littlefield, 2006.

Mélonio, Françoise. *Tocqueville and the French.* Translated by Beth G. Raps. Charlottesville, VA: University Press of Virginia, 1998. (First published as *Tocqueville et les Français* [Paris: Aubier, 1993].)

Pierson, George Wilson. *Tocqueville and Beaumont in America.* New York: Oxford University Press, 1938.

Schleifer, James T. *The Making of Tocqueville's "Democracy in America."* 2nd rev. ed. Indianapolis: Liberty Fund, 2000. (1st ed.: Chapel Hill: University of North Carolina Press, 1980.)

Tocqueville. *Democracy in America.* Edited and translated by Harvey C. Mansfield and Delba Winthrop. Chicago: University of Chicago Press, 2000.

———. *Democracy in America*. Edited by Eduardo Nolla. Translated by James T. Schleifer. Bilingual French-English, historical-critical edition. 4 vols. Indianapolis: Liberty Fund, 2010.

———. *Journey to America*. Edited by J. P. Mayer. Translated by George Lawrence. New Haven: Yale University Press, 1960. (Tocqueville's complete travel notebooks)

Welch, Cheryl. *De Tocqueville*. New York: Oxford University Press, 2001.

Zunz, Olivier, ed. *Alexis de Tocqueville and Gustave de Beaumont in America: Their Friendship and Their Travels*. Translated by Arthur Goldhammer. Charlottesville: University of Virginia Press, 2010.

NOTES

INTRODUCTION

1. *Democracy in America*, Harvey C. Mansfield and Delba Winthrop, eds. and trans. (Chicago: University of Chicago Press, 2000), 7; hereafter cited as *Democracy* (UCP).

2. See below, Suggestions for Further Reading.

CHAPTER ONE

1. Two extensive biographies are available in English: André Jardin, *Tocqueville: A Biography*, Lydia Davis, trans. (New York: Farrar, Straus and Giroux, 1988); and Hugh Brogan, *Alexis de Tocqueville: A Life* (New Haven: Yale University Press, 2007).

2. Olivier Zunz and Alan Kahan, eds. and trans., *The Tocqueville Reader: A Life in Letters and Politics* (Oxford: Blackwell, 2002), 336: letter to Sophie Swetchine, February 26, 1857.

3. Olivier Zunz, ed., and Arthur Goldhammer, trans., *Alexis de Tocqueville and Gustave de Beaumont in America: Their Friendship and Their Travels* (Charlottesville: University of Virginia Press, 2010), 573 (hereafter cited as *Tocqueville and Beaumont*): letter to Henry Reeve, March 22, 1837.

4. Roger Boesche, ed., James Toupin and Roger Boesche, trans., *Alexis de Tocqueville: Selected Letters on Politics and Society* (Berkeley: University of California Press, 1985), 62–64 (hereafter cited as *Selected Letters*): letter to Charles Stoffels, October 22, 1831.

5. *Democracy* (UCP), especially 511–14.

6. *Selected Letters*, 325–26 and 348–49: letters to Sophie Swetchine, January 7 and February 11, 1856.

CHAPTER TWO

1. For details of the American journey, see the classic, almost day-by-day study by George Wilson Pierson, *Tocqueville and Beaumont in America* (New York: Oxford University Press, 1938); and the recent shorter account by Leo Damrosch, *Tocqueville's Discovery of America* (New York: Farrar, Straus and Giroux, 2010).

2. For Tocqueville's own account of his and Beaumont's frontier experience, "A Fortnight in the Wilderness," published only after his death, see *Democracy in America*, Eduardo Nolla, ed., and James T. Schleifer, trans. (Indianapolis: Liberty Fund, 2010), 4 vols., 4:1303–59; hereafter cited as *Democracy in America* (LF).

3. For English translations of Tocqueville's travel notebooks, see *Tocqueville and Beau-*

mont, part 2, 209–393 (substantial excerpts); and *Journey to America*, J. P. Mayer, ed., and George Lawrence, trans. (New Haven: Yale University Press, 1960); hereafter cited as *Journey*. For translations of Tocqueville's letters, see especially *Tocqueville and Beaumont* and *Selected Letters*; some of Beaumont's letters appear in *Tocqueville and Beaumont*, part 1.

4. *Tocqueville and Beaumont*, 447: letter to Le Peletier d'Aunay, June 7, 1831.

5. Ibid., 24: letter to Edouard de Tocqueville, May 28, 1831.

6. The author of *Commentaries on American Law*, James Kent, was a well-known jurist, former chief justice of the supreme court of New York, and an important influence on Tocqueville's understanding of American laws and the Constitution.

7. Jared Sparks, American historian, famous especially for his books on George Washington and the colonial and revolutionary periods, was one of the most significant American sources for Tocqueville on the issues of American decentralization (local liberties and towns) and tyranny of the majority.

8. *Tocqueville and Beaumont*, 446–47: letter to Le Peletier d'Aunay, June 7, 1831.

9. Ibid.

10. Ibid., 204–5: letter to his brother, Edouard, January 20, 1832.

11. See "Sources Cited by Tocqueville," *Democracy* (UCP), 705–9; also Eduardo Nolla's even more complete listing, "Works Used by Tocqueville," which includes items drawn from the working papers, as well as the text and notes, of Tocqueville's book, in *Democracy in America* (LF), 4:1377–95.

12. See, for example, Sean Wilentz, *Society, Politics, and the Market Revolution, 1815–1848* (Washington, DC: AHA, 1990); and consult the full histories by Wilentz, *The Rise of American Democracy: Jefferson to Lincoln* (New York: W. W. Norton, 2005) (The title itself is a tribute to Tocqueville); and Daniel Walker Howe, *What Hath God Wrought: The Transformation of America, 1815–1848* (New York: Oxford University Press, 2007).

13. *Democracy in America* (LF), 1:85–86, notes d and e, from the original working manuscript and drafts.

14. *Democracy* (UCP), 374–76.

15. See Wilentz, *Rise of American Democracy*, especially chaps. 9–14, and his presentations of the ideas of many prominent individuals.

16. *Tocqueville and Beaumont*, 563: letter to Camille d'Orglandes, November 29, 1834.

17. *Selected Letters*, 38: letter to Chabrol, June 9, 1831.

18. Ibid., 61: letter to Chabrol, October 7, 1831.

19. Ibid., 57–58: letter to Louis de Kergorlay, June 29, 1831.

20. *Tocqueville and Beaumont*, 205: letter to Hervé de Tocqueville, January 24, 1832.

21. See especially James T. Schleifer, *The Making of Tocqueville's "Democracy in America,"* 2nd rev. ed. (Indianapolis: Liberty Fund, 2000), chaps. 1 and 2; hereafter cited as *Making*.

22. See *Democracy* (UCP), 27–45; and consult Tocqueville's own long bibliographic note on pp. 683–89.

23. Gustave de Beaumont, *Marie, ou l'esclavage aux Etats-Unis: Tableau des moeurs américaines*, 2 vols. (Paris: Gosselin, 1835). Beaumont's work was a pioneering study of American slavery and racism and enjoyed some success. But the book suffered, first, from an awkward blend of forms (part romantic novel and part detached analysis), and second, from comparison with Tocqueville's masterpiece. No American translation appeared until 1958.

24. *Making*, 31 and 32: letters to Beaumont, November 22, 1836; and to Kergorlay, November 10, 1836.

25. See the opening two chapters of the 1840 portion; *Democracy* (UCP), 403–10.

26. *Making*, 39–40; Tocqueville's emphasis.

27. *Democracy* (UCP), 479–82.

28. *Making*, 44: letters to Beaumont, October 23, 1839; and November 2, 1839; Tocqueville's emphasis.

29. *Tocqueville and Beaumont*, 587: letter to Kergorlay, October 18, 1847.

30. *Making*, 3: letter to Eugène Stoffels, February 21, 1831; Tocqueville's emphasis.

31. *Making*, 8–9.

32. *Democracy* (UCP), 302–96.

33. See ibid., 298–302; for "Conclusion," see 391–96.

34. Ibid., 3–15.

35. *Making*, 28.

36. Ibid., 29: letter to Reeve, June 5, 1836; Tocqueville's emphasis.

37. Ibid., 37.

38. *Democracy* (UCP), "Notice," 399–400.

39. *Making*, 36–37.

CHAPTER THREE

1. *Democracy* (UCP), 6.

2. Ibid., 7.

3. *Democracy* (LF), 1:28, note n, from the drafts.

4. *Democracy* (UCP), 275; and see 292, note 8.

5. Ibid., 358.

6. Ibid., 27–45.

7. *Making*, 8–9.

8. *Democracy* (UCP), 675–76; and see Tocqueville's 1840 chapter on historians in democratic times, 469–72.

9. For fuller discussion, see *Making*, 89–94.

10. Ibid., 79–80.

11. Ibid., 80.

12. Ibid., 28.

CHAPTER FOUR

1. *Democracy* (UCP), 3.

2. Ibid., 3.

3. Ibid., 3–6.

4. Ibid., 45.

5. Ibid., 52.

6. Ibid., 546–53, especially 550, in the chapter on relationships between servant and master.

7. *Democracy* (LF), 3:692, note e, from the drafts.

8. *Democracy* (UCP), 47; and see 47–50.

9. *Democracy* (LF), 1:75–76, from the original working manuscript; my emphasis.

10. *Making*, 332–33.

11. Ibid., 330.

12. *Democracy* (UCP), 7; and see 301–2.

13. For further discussion of the meanings of democracy, see *Making,* 329–34.

14. For these three portraits, see *Democracy* (UCP), 7–12.

15. Ibid., 10.

16. Ibid., 12.

17. Ibid., 42.

18. Ibid., 43.

19. Ibid., 670.

20. *Making,* 303; Tocqueville's own emphasis.

21. *Democracy* (UCP), 293–94.

22. For a similar insistence that true liberty must be understood as promotion of the broadest possible participation in public life, consult the book by supreme court justice Stephen Breyer, *Active Liberty: Interpreting Our Democratic Constitution* (New York: Knopf, 2005).

23. *Democracy* (UCP), 52.

24. Ibid., 480.

25. Ibid., 482.

26. Ibid., 189.

27. Ibid., 511–14, "Why the Americans Show Themselves So Restive in the Midst of Their Well-Being."

28. Ibid., 644–45.

29. Ibid., 639–40, "Equality Naturally Gives Men the Taste for Free Institutions."

30. Ibid., 481.

CHAPTER FIVE

1. *Selected Letters,* 39: letter to Ernest de Chabrol, June 9, 1831.

2. *Journey,* 245; and see 69, 234, and 260.

3. *Democracy* (UCP), 272–73.

4. See ibid., vol. 2, part 1, chaps. 3, 4, and 9.

5. Ibid., especially 385–88.

6. Ibid., vol. 2, part 2, chaps. 10 and 11.

7. Ibid., 506–7.

8. Ibid., 509.

9. Ibid., 514–17.

10. Ibid., 515–16; and see 643–44.

11. Ibid., 482.

12. *Making,* 308–9.

13. *Democracy* (UCP), 482–83.

14. Ibid., 233.

15. For the exchange, see *Making,* 307.

16. Ibid., 318.

17. Ibid.

18. *Democracy* (UCP), 301.

19. *Making,* 313, from the original working manuscript.

20. *Democracy* (UCP), 672.

21. Ibid., 53 and 55.

22. *Democracy* (LF), 2:412, note s, from the drafts.

23. *Democracy* (UCP), 248.

24. Ibid., 145; and see 84–85.

25. *Democracy* (LF), 2:411, note o, from the drafts. In the 1835 text itself, see *Democracy* (UCP), 248–49.

26. *Democracy* (UCP), 91–92; my emphasis.

27. Ibid., 82.

28. Ibid., 82–83; for the 1840 portrait, see 662–63.

29. Ibid., 88.

30. Ibid., 301; and see 301–302.

31. Ibid., 52.

32. *Making,* 195–96.

33. *Democracy* (UCP), 298–302.

34. *Making,* 199–200.

35. *Democracy* (UCP), 299.

36. Ibid., 301; and see 302.

37. *Making,* 198–99: letter to Kergorlay, January 1835.

38. *Democracy* (UCP), 145.

39. *Making,* 248.

40. *Democracy* (UCP), 235–49 and 250–64.

41. Ibid., 235.

42. Ibid., 237.

43. Ibid., 248, Tocqueville's note 6.

44. Ibid., 242.

45. Ibid., 241–42, Tocqueville's note 4.

46. Ibid., 241.

47. Ibid., 244–45.

48. Ibid., 240; and see 379–80.

49. Ibid., 246.

50. Ibid., 247.

51. Ibid., 409.

52. *Democracy* (LF), 3:721, note r, from the drafts.

53. *Democracy* (UCP), 410.

54. This perspective on tyranny of the majority, especially as it relates to race, is perhaps the central theme of Beaumont's *Marie* (1835).

55. *Democracy* (UCP), 530–32.

56. Ibid., 479.

57. Ibid., 649; and see 703–4, Tocqueville's note XXVI.

58. *Democracy* (LF), 4:1253–54, note o, from the drafts.

59. Ibid., 4:1247, note d, from the drafts.

60. *Democracy* (UCP), 661.

61. Ibid., 662.

62. *Making,* 210.

63. *Democracy* (UCP), 515.

64. Ibid., 663.

65. *Democracy* (LF), 4:1255, note p, from the drafts.

66. *Democracy* (UCP), 647–48; the quote is from the drafts, see *Democracy* (LF), 4:1212, note k.

67. *Democracy* (UCP), 241.

CHAPTER SIX

1. *Democracy* (LF), 3:871, note a, from the drafts; Tocqueville's emphasis.
2. *Democracy* (UCP), 666.
3. Ibid., 666–73.
4. *Making,* 163: letter to Hervé de Tocqueville, June 3, 1831.
5. *Democracy* (UCP), 67.
6. Ibid., 82–93.
7. *Journey,* 252.
8. *Democracy* (UCP), 180.
9. Ibid., 180–81.
10. Ibid.
11. Ibid., 183–84.
12. Ibid., 490 and 492.
13. Ibid., 668.
14. Ibid., 491.
15. *Selected Letters,* 38: letter to Ernest de Chabrol, June 9, 1831.
16. *Democracy* (UCP), 62; and see 358–59.
17. *Making,* 294; also see *Democracy* (UCP), 225–27.
18. *Tocqueville and Beaumont,* 332–33: Sing Sing, May 29, 1831.
19. *Democracy* (LF), 2:509, note a, from the drafts.
20. See for example *Democracy* (UCP), 225–27 and 358–59.
21. Ibid., 501; and see 500–503 and 514–17.
22. Ibid., 538.
23. Ibid., 502–3.
24. Ibid., 27–45.
25. Ibid., 43.
26. Ibid., 282.
27. Ibid., 275–88; also 405–6 and 417–24.
28. Ibid., 287–88.
29. Ibid., 520–21; and see 417–24.
30. See for example ibid., 417–24.
31. *Selected Letters,* 294–95: letter to Corcelle, September 17, 1853.
32. Tocqueville did not always praise religion as the handmaiden of liberty, however. In the 1835 *Democracy,* he explicitly disagreed with Montesquieu's idea that fear was the principle of despotism; Tocqueville argued that religion, not fear, sustained despotic nations; see *Democracy* (UCP), 89.
33. *Democracy* (UCP), 302.
34. *Selected Letters,* 112–15: letter to Eugène Stoffels, October 5, 1836.
35. *Democracy* (UCP), 302.
36. *Tocqueville and Beaumont,* 583–84: letter to Reeve, February 3, 1840; Tocqueville's emphasis.
37. *Democracy* (LF), 4:1278–79, note b; compare *Democracy* (UCP), 673–76.
38. *Democracy* (LF), 4:1275–76, note y, from the drafts.
39. *Democracy* (UCP), 7.

CHAPTER SEVEN

1. On this topic, see especially: Seymour Drescher, ed., *Tocqueville and Beaumont on Social Reform* (New York: Harper and Row, 1968); Michael Drolet, *Tocqueville, Democracy*

and Social Reform (New York: Palgrave Macmillan, 2003); and Richard Swedberg, *Tocqueville's Political Economy* (Princeton: Princeton University Press, 2009).

2. *Tocqueville and Beaumont*, 363–65.

3. Ibid., 249: conversation with Robert Vaux, October 27, 1831.

4. For these working papers, see *Democracy* (LF), 1:81, note s; 1:85, note d; and 4:1237–38, note a; and see *Democracy* (UCP), 655–58.

5. *Democracy* (UCP), 530–32; and see 556–57.

6. Ibid., 399.

7. *Making*, 110.

8. See, for example, *Democracy* (UCP), 649 and 667.

9. *Tocqueville and Beaumont*, 364–65.

10. See especially the working papers for part 4 of the 1840 portion; *Democracy* (LF), 4:1221–44.

11. *Democracy* (UCP), 90; and see 231–35.

12. *Democracy* (LF), 3:869–70, note h.

13. Ibid., 3:903–4.

14. Ibid., 4:1235–37, note y.

15. *Democracy* (UCP), 667.

16. *Democracy* (LF), 4:1215, note p.

17. During the writing of his *Democracy* in the 1830s, and especially by the late 1830s, Tocqueville was closely involved in four major public issues, in each case advocating decisive use of governmental power: to reform the penitentiary system, to address the causes of poverty, to colonize Algeria, and to abolish slavery. Each of these measures, he realized, required a strong and active central government.

18. *Democracy* (LF), 4:1079, note m, from the drafts.

19. *Democracy* (UCP), 479–82 and 639–40.

20. *Selected Letters*, 100–102: letter to John Stuart Mill, June 1835.

21. Ibid., 98–99: letter to Eugène Stoffels, February 21, 1835; and compare *Democracy* (UCP), 234–35.

22. *Democracy* (UCP), 298–302 and 673–76, "General View of the Subject"; also see 234–35.

23. Ibid., 674.

24. Ibid., 674–75.

25. *Tocqueville and Beaumont*, 310.

26. *Democracy* (UCP), 245.

27. Ibid., 428.

28. Ibid., 430.

29. *Making*, 285.

30. *Democracy* (UCP), 432.

31. Ibid.

32. Ibid., 432–33.

33. Ibid., 663.

34. *Democracy* (LF), 4:1144–45, note q.

35. Ibid.

36. *Democracy* (UCP), 616–17.

37. Ibid., 599; and see the entire chapter on honor, 589–99.

38. Ibid., 558–63.

39. Ibid., 565.

40. Ibid., 576.

41. *Democracy* (LF), 3:886, note c, from the drafts.

42. *Democracy* (UCP), 187.

43. Ibid., 670–71.

44. See, on apathy, ibid., 704, Tocqueville's note XXVII.

45. Ibid., 620–21.

46. Tocqueville made other significant remarks about this topic. As nations become democratic, he wrote, they become more alike, and among similar democratic nations war becomes more rare. If war occurs, however, it will be more general, involving opposing coalitions of nations, and more total, engaging the entire population. He also asserted that democratic nations were more vulnerable at the outbreak of a conflict, but once at war, were harder to defeat in the long run. See especially, *Democracy* (UCP), vol. 2, part 3, chaps. 22–26.

47. *Democracy* (LF), 2:344, note y; and see *Democracy* (UCP), 28 and 205.

48. *Democracy* (LF), 3:690–91, note c.

49. *Democracy* (UCP), 193, 426–28, and 508–9.

50. Ibid., 215–16 and 219–20.

51. Ibid., 189–90 and 297.

52. See for example ibid., 511–13.

53. Ibid., 189, 270–71, 297, 511–14, and 644–45.

54. Ibid., 270–71, 297, and 511–14, "Why the Americans Show Themselves So Restive in the Midst of Their Well-Being"; and note that the spiritual restlessness of human beings was a theme also found by Tocqueville in Pascal.

55. *Democracy* (LF), 3:693, note f, from the drafts for Tocqueville's 1840 foreword; Tocqueville's emphasis.

56. Ibid., 4:1281, note e; Tocqueville's emphasis.

CHAPTER EIGHT

1. See *Democracy* (UCP), 19–27, the opening chapter of the 1835 *Democracy*, entitled "External Configuration of North America"; and consult *Making*, chaps. 3 and 4.

2. *Democracy* (UCP), 146–49, esp. 147; also see, from the chapter on the government of the states, 56. Although Tocqueville found the American theory innovative, he did not believe that federalism was applicable to France.

3. *Making*, 125, from the original working manuscript.

4. *Democracy* (UCP), 149.

5. Ibid., 257.

6. *Democracy* (LF), 1:167, note b.

7. *Democracy* (UCP), 191–92 and 236.

8. Ibid., 118.

9. See ibid., 302–25, on Native Americans; and 302–7 and 326–48, on blacks.

10. Ibid., 366.

11. Ibid., 348.

12. Tocqueville returned to American racism in the 1840 *Democracy*; see ibid., 538–39.

13. See Tocqueville's impressive summary of those issues, ibid., 370–79.

14. See the subsection on the topic, ibid., 348–79.

15. Ibid., 362–63 and 370–71; also consult *Making*, chaps. 7–9, especially chap. 8.

16. *Making*, 36–37.

17. *Selected Letters*, 46–47: letter to Kergorlay, June 29, 1831.

18. *Democracy* (UCP), 379–80; and see 379–84.

19. *Democracy* (LF), 2:561, from the original working manuscript.

20. *Democracy* (UCP), 395–96.

CHAPTER NINE

1. *Selected Letters,* 99–100: letter to Eugène Stoffels, February 21, 1835.

2. Ibid., 115: letter to Henry Reeve, March 22, 1837.

INDEX

The following is primarily a name index; for most topics and themes, see the Glossary and the Guide to Key Chapters and Passages.